Research on Socialization of Young Children
in the Nordic Countries

Research on Socialization
of Young Children
in the Nordic Countries

An annotated and selected bibliography

Edited by
Berit Elgaard, Ole Langsted and Dion Sommer

AARHUS UNIVERSITY PRESS

Copyright: Aarhus University Press, 1989
Printed in Denmark by AKA-Print, Aarhus
ISBN 87 7288 175 5

AARHUS UNIVERSITY PRESS
Aarhus University
DK-8000 Aarhus C, Denmark

LIST OF CONTENTS

Societal Development in Relation to Young Children
in Contemporary Nordic Countries – An overview .... p. 25

References and sources .... p. 29

Part II: Bibliography

RESEARCH TEAM

The research team comprises social science oriented researchers representing various behavioural disciplines.

Project leader

Lars Dencik

Institute of Economics and Planning
Roskilde University
Postboks 260
DK-4000 Roskilde
Denmark

Tel.: 45-2-75 77 11

National research groups:

Denmark

Ole Langsted
Dion Sommer

Institute of Psychology
University of Aarhus
Asylvej 4
DK 8240 Risskov
Denmark
Tel.: 45-6-17 55 11

Finland

Anja Riitta Lahikainen
Harriet Strandell

Department of Social Psychology
University of Helsinki
Fabiankatu 28A
SF-00 100 Helsinki
Finland
Tel.: 358-0-650 211

Iceland

Sigurjón Björnsson
Baldur Kristjánsson

Faculty of Social Sciences
Háskóli Islands
Oddi v./Sudurgata
IS-101 Reykjavik
Iceland
Tel.: 354-1-2 50 88

Norway

Agnes Andenæs
Hanne Haavind

Institute of Psychology
University of Trondheim
N-7005 Dragvoll
Norway
Tel.: 47-7-92 04 11

Sweden

Gunilla Dahlberg
Berit Ljung

Department of
Educational Research
Stockholm Institute of Education
Box 34 103
S-100 26 Stockholm
Sweden
Tel.: 46-8-22 16 80

Editors of the Bibliography

Berit Elgaard
Ole Langsted
Dion Sommer

Institute of Psychology
University of Aarhus
Asylvej 4
DK-8240 Risskov
Tel.: 45-6-17 55 11

INTRODUCTION

The welfare debate led today in the Nordic countries - *Denmark, Finland, Iceland, Norway* and *Sweden* - has gathered much attention in international societal circles. Sociologists and psychologists have been wondering about the consequences of the social equalising- and social welfare being linked together as in "the Scandinavian model". With astonishment, now and then admiration and trembling, respectively, political debaters have referred to the connection between individual and society, society and family, as well as parents and children in the Nordic countries. Much has been assumed - less known.

A reason for this lack of knowledge is that a lot of the research showing results about peoples' everyday life has only been accessible in some of the Nordic languages - and consequently inaccessible to the international public being interested.

Especially the conditions in the Nordic countries concerning the child's situation in family and society has been of interest to the international public.

The aim of the project *"Childhood, Society, and Development in the Nordic Countries"* is to grasp the distinctive features in the construction of modern childhood in order to understand its influence on the socialisation of young children in the five Nordic countries.

How to describe the natural settings in which young children in the Nordic countries are to be found? What are the distinctive features of those settings, as perceived from a social psychological perspective? What are the characteristics of the social interactional processes in which the children participate? Many young children spend their days in different environments (e.g. nursery, kindergarten, family) how do these different sectors influence each other? In other words: How is the overall picture of the everyday life of young children in the Nordic countries put together today? What kind of cultural similarities do we find and what are the important differences?

The research project focuses on mapping the children's socialisation situation as a whole. In the terminology of the project this is defined as the sum of the children's social experiences in their natural settings as well as experiences of the interaction between those settings.

This provides us with the following theoretical basis:

The child is created as the person he/she is in the social psychological sense of the word through his/her interactions in his/her different social settings. But the particular experience gained by the child by those interactions is given its specific psychological significance by the other parts of his/her experience gained simultaneously in another sphere of life. The insights derived by the child on the basis of this complex process of social interaction become important to both his/her social and mental processing in the future. But the course of the interactional processes is directed in a decisive way by its structural conditions prevailing for the actors of the interaction.

Although the everyday life of today's children may seem fragmented, it always constitutes a *whole*. This entity gives meaning to the child of the separate social experiences that the child makes in the various spheres of life.

The approach of the investigation is *holistic*. The behavioural and psychological phenomena observed are explained on the basis of the *context* in which they appear. The sources of the explanations are above all the predicaments, i.e., the *material, social and cultural conditions*, prevailing in such situations where these phenomena are to be found.

The construction of childhood is sensitive to change in both time and space, i.e. there are both historically and geographically induced variations in its outline. In other words: Childhood is not inalterable, but changes along with the evolution of the society.

In the last few decades, people's way of life has undergone very rapid and radical transformations in the Nordic countries. New technologies have created new opportunities for many people, new productive factors have developed new working conditions, and a changed distribution of the labour market, bringing about new patterns in the social and service sectors. Family patterns within the social and service sectors have been subjected to alterations. Family patterns, life styles, and also life orientations have been exposed to alternations [1].

---

[1]   This has been documented in the series of books about young children's living conditions being published within the frame of the project "Childhood, Society, and Devel-

The corresponding changes in people's everyday life create new developmental conditions. The important question posed by this study is to discover in which way these conditions are linked together and how they constitute the complete living-space formed by *modern childhood*. How is this living-space structured for children? Which is the social experience gained by children in this space? How do they mentally process such experience? And how does it shape the child's social competence, cognitive categorisation and emotional disposition?

These main factors are investigated in the project and comparisons are made cross-culturally between the five Nordic countries[2].

* * *

The first part of this book comprises a review article by *Lars Dencik*, *Ole Langsted* and *Dion Sommer*, describing the main traits of young children's material, social and cultural upbringing conditions in the Nordic societies today.

The second part comprises an annotated Nordic bibliography of selected research within this field.

Being selective, this publication does not claim to include all titles, existing within the field - on the contrary, the selecting criteria are tight. The selection has been made by the researchers connected to the project.

The following lines of direction in connection with the inclusion, exclusion and insertion of literature have been followed:

In this bibliography the *selection* of research is based on the main interests of the research project "Childhood, Society and Development in the Nordic Countries" which are to *grasp the distinctive features in*

---

opment in the Nordic Countries": Andenæs, A. & H. Haavind (1987). Små barns livsvilkår i Norge/Young Children's Living Conditions in Norway, Oslo: Universitetsforlaget., Langsted, O. & D. Sommer (1988). Småbørns livsvilkår i Danmark/Youngs Children's Living Conditions in Denmark, Copenhagen: Hans Reitzels Forlag. Lainhikainen, A. R. & H. Strandell (1988). Lapsen kasvuehdot Suomessa/Young Childre's Living Conditions in Finland, Helsinki: Gaudeamus. Corresponding material about the conditions in Iceland and Sweden are planned to be published as books in 1989.

2   The results of the project, will be a systematic comparative analysis of the content of selected 5 year old children's everyday life in the five countries. The analysis will be published in 1990 as a monograph with the preliminary title "Modern Childhood: On the Everyday Life of Young Children in the Nordic Welfare States."

the construction of modern childhood in order to understand its influence on the socialisation of young children in the five Nordic countries.

Only academical research, "para"-academical or public statements mainly with an empirical basis in the respective countries will be registered. Books, reports and articles from periodicals are included. Only public accessible publications within the decade 1974-1985 have been selected. The focus is on "normal" children, i.e. research of deviative and ill children has not been included.

The following search terms have been used: Young children (0-6 year-olds), young children's living conditions and socialisation, ideology, culture and young children, social interaction and young children.

The material is presented for each separate country involved. The five countries appear in alphabetical order. Within the countries the publications have been categorised according to the kind of socialisation conditions that the research mainly treats. Either within *"Young children's material conditions"* referring to the physical and economic frame, within *"Young children's social conditions"* referring to the social relationships that make up the child's living-space, or within *"Young children's cultural conditions"* referring to the ideological content conveyed in the child's living space. Each publication was read before categorised. Concerning Iceland, the literature has not been categorised on account of the few references.

If more titles have been published in connection with a particular research project only the most essential ones have been incorporated.

The choice of a specific insertion has been an evaluation of how to stress the main contents in a certain project/publication.

The references are presented with reference to a model containing *bibliographic citations*, a brief *summary*, information about the *theoretical frame of reference*, a description of the *method employed*, and of the *results*. In very few cases where the results have not been presented, the reason may be that the publication is an antology or the results so many that they are impossible to refer.

A cross-sectional subject index has been elaborated as a supplement to the main categories. Furthermore an author index is available in the book.

* * *

The edition of the bibliography was carried through at the Institute of Psychology, Aarhus University, and conducted by *Berit Elgaard*, *Ole Langsted* and *Dion Sommer*.

Project leader *Lars Dencik* participated from the very beginning in the organising and planning of this work. His suggestions and advice have been important in the production of this bibliography.

In Finland *Anja Riita Lahikainen* and *Ilse Cantell* have been the editors, and in Iceland *Signe Klara Hannesdóttir*. In the other Nordic countries the project collaborators have participated in the selection and they have had the responsibility of examining and approving of their national part of the bibliography. The annotation has been made by *Berit Elgaard*.

Without the help from the following persons, this bibliography would not have been published: We thank *Lone Hansen* for her assistance in connection with the lay-out of the book, *Annie Dolmer Nielsen* for the graphical lay-out and *John McLaughlin* for the translation of the manuscript into English.

The project *"Childhood, Society and Development in the Nordic Countries"* has been financed by the Joint Committee of the Nordic Social Science Research Council. The publication also received financial support from the Nordic Cultural Fund, the Institute of Psychology, Aarhus University, The Danish Research Council for The Humanities, and The Danish Social Science Research Council.

Aarhus, February 1989

PART I

MODERN CHILDHOOD IN THE NORDIC COUNTRIES: MATERIAL, SOCIAL AND CULTURAL ASPECTS

Lars Dencik, Ole Langsted and Dion Sommer

Modern Childhood

Childhood is the life-space during which children live and develop. This life-space is changeable and its form variable, seen both from the historical and the class perspective. In other words, today's children in the Nordic Countries generally live a childhood different from that lived by children only a few decades ago. Childhood is also formed differently depending on where - within a society's social structure - one is born.

Childhood is not what it used to be. Adults' experience of conditions from their own growing up, do not constitute reality for today's preschool children. Consequently, parents', pedagogues', decision makers' and other adults' experience cannot be applied directly as frames within which young children's lives and growing up today can be understood.

The children are subjected to a childhood that is formed and changed according to society's development. Conceptions about children's "nature", "needs", or "optimal conditions of growing up", change accordingly. Thus the child's development does not proceed, as traditional developmental psychology tends to see it, independently of the society and the cultural relations that the preschool child is part of.

A great deal of literature has been pursued in recent years which, without necessarily being in agreement, attempts to understand the relation between societal development and changes in children's conditions. Some, inspired by Phillipe Ariès' (1962) pioneer work on the very early days of childhood, and developmental history, have emphasised what the child has lost as a result of industrialisation - especially in connection with the child's entering into meaningful relations in society. Others like Edward Shorter (1975) have confined themselves to this in their studies of how children in earlier times, have been treated and mistreated by their nearest and dearest. The increased respect and consideration in modern times, for the child's special background as a being which is not the same as an adults'. This is perceived as a result of societal development which, also according to Shorter, created the social conditions for the "sentiments" that bind the modern nuclear family together and not least, historically created the strong emotional relations in the family between parents and children.

Most recently, a number of researchers (for example Neil Postman, 1984) have pointed out a new tendency towards erasure of the borderlines between the adults' life and area of experience and those of the child. This process of erasure is taking place by power of the development of new technology and media. According to this analysis, childhood in modern - or perhaps more accurately, postmodern - society, is gradually being dissolved.

Despite the fact that the above analyses reach such different conclusions, there is one common feature that characterises them: The insight that the life-space in society which constitutes childhood, is changeable across time and space. In other words, that childhood is not constant - it changes as a function of societal development.

But how is childhood changed and what consequences does it have for the children growing up under the new conditions? It is such questions as these that this article will attempt to give some answers to, with respect to the development of 0-6 year-old children in the Nordic countries.

In recent years, the highly developed industrialised countries have undergone a rapid and drastic change, attended by decisive consequences for people's living conditions, ways of living together and way of life. Children's lives have been decisively affected through the influence that new production methods, new technology and new working conditions, as well as changed norms for living together and upbringing, have had on adults. One can say that childhood is created, not by children, but for children. It is the adults who - more or less consciously controlled - form, plan, and regulate the framework of the life that becomes our children's. One particularly decisive consequence for young children's growing up in the Nordic countries is the social changes that intervene in the parents' dispositions and daily life. An investigation of connections existing between society and parents with young children is therefore of vital importance. The relation between societal development and children's development can be illustrated through the below model.

Figure 1: Societal development and development of children

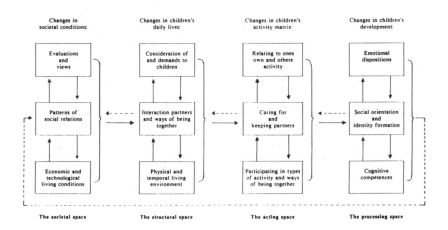

Young children are independent, active small human beings who are capable of causing changes within their own environment. But they must act within the "space" which their societally and adult-regulated agents structure for them. What determines that little Lissa has to "expand" outside the family circle on week days and at home at weekends are, for example, daddy's and mummy's working hours and the rules that regulate their work. In other words, there is a close connection between young children's conditions of growing up and pertinent aspects of the functioning of modern society.

In order to be able to acquire more thorough knowledge about young children's living conditions in our society, a concrete analysis will be needed. We have chosen three central perspectives around which to organise our data.

3 (Part I)

- The material perspective, describing the chronological, physical and economic frames around the child's life.
- The social perspective, presenting the modern conditions for the child's social interactions.
- The cultural perspective, concerning the ideological, norm-determined climate surrounding today's young child.

The purpose is, on the basis of the above three main areas, to analyse the industrial and welfare society's social psychological consequences for the child, and to discuss what new living conditions are characteristic of childhood in the Nordic countries.

Young Children's Material Living Conditions

Generally, young children in the Nordic countries live under materially secure conditions. There are almost no cases of children being hungry and in general, children live in modern, well equipped housing where they very often have their own bedrooms.

It is possible for anyone to get help and support from society through the social security system, if the parents are unable to support the child.

Child mortality is among the lowest in the world and children are generally healthy and well fed. Children's material conditions are mainly guaranteed by the parents' paid work.

The Parents' Working Conditions

Changes in the life style of the family with children are closely connected with the parents working conditions. Economy and material standard of living are inseparably bound up with the extreme changes in the woman's relation to the labour market, in particular. 20-25 years ago, a family would normally have to be supported at the standard that was acceptable on basis of the man's 48 hour, contractually determined working week. Today, it is a typical feature that the parents work jointly. Figure 2 illustrates this for men and women in four of the Nordic countries.

Figure 2: Employed men and women age 25 - 34. 1983.

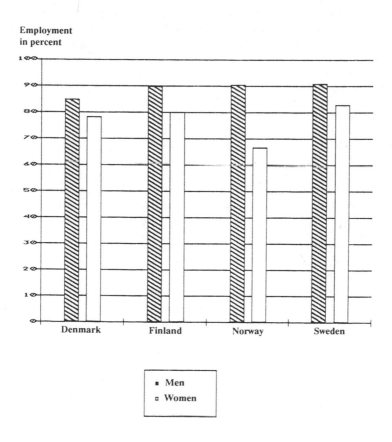

Source: Yearbook of Nordic Statistics 1984, p. 81.

As will be seen, the proportion of employed with respect to both men and women in 1983, is approximately the same in Denmark, Finland, and Sweden. For example, the proportion of working **mothers** with children under 7 years of age in Sweden, has risen during the past 10 years from 57% to 83%. Only Norway differs with a somewhat lower percentage for women.

In the North, this development has been taking place during the last 25 years and has continued constantly until today, in the second half of the 80's. This upheaval has had considerable consequences for the whole family's material and social life.

Unlike her mother, the modern woman does not diminish her engagement in life outside the family, when she has very small children. On the contrary, today young women with small children show a clear tendency to maintain their ties to the labour market.

This marked historical shift naturally leads to a series of consequences with regard to the roles traditionally played by women. For example, we see during the 1980's that there are not only more mothers of small children who work outside the home than there were ten years before, but also that the proportion of housewives today is less than a tenth as opposed to almost one half in the middle of the seventies. In the space of a short time span, the social category "housewife" has almost ceased to exist in the North, except in Norway, where half of the women are still housewives.

Furthermore, parents to young children in the North, generally work more than others. However, men's working hours have decreased to around 40 hours, whereas women's working hours have increased. Many mothers to young children work 30 or more hours and the family's total number of working hours outside the home has therefore risen. To the child, this means that it spends more time together with its father and less with its mother. That is to say, there is a tendency towards a more equal division of the time spent by the child between the mother and the father, than was earlier the case. This also means that being together with the parents is placed at certain times during the 24 hour period, when mummy and daddy are home from work.

Sharing Housework and Childcare

In order to evaluate the parents work situation, it must, of course, be viewed as a whole. This means that the combination of work outside the home, as well as the division of housework (including childcare), must be included in order to acquire a fairer picture of how the time factor sets the framework for and organises the way of being together. Housework, as well as parts of childcare work in all of the Nordic countries, is a matter of concern for the child's parents.

With the increase in the woman's participation in work outside the family, families throughout the 60's and up until today have been confronted with a new problem: The redistribution of tasks within the family framework.

Two conditions come to mind immediately, when one is faced with the task of examining the changes that took place in the family in the period in which women's frequency of employment began to increase: 1) The total time used on housework fell. 2) The man's participation rose slightly in the same period. However, there is no indication of equal division of housework or childcare. The woman still takes responsibility for most of the tasks in the home and uses most time on them.

It seems, then, that the *norms* for housework have changed: One does not vacuum clean so often any more and the dust on the sideboard is allowed to stay there longer. For example, until the mother-in-law is coming to visit. It is possible that the marked consumption by the family with children of kitchen hardware, has contributed to a reduction of the total amount of time used on housework.

It is interesting that the same tendency towards a reduction of the time used on keeping house, is the case in all the Nordic countries. For example, mothers to young children in Norway today, do less housework than before. On the other hand, however, they spend more time on the child. The Norwegian family with young children gives a higher priority to being together with the child, than to keeping house and cleaning. This shows interesting historical tendencies, where the child itself and its needs have become more visible. We see the same tendency in Finland as in Norway and Denmark: The Finnish mothers have also adapted to the fact that they are at work for most of the day. They solve the problems that arise, first and foremost by reducing the extent of the practical tasks in the family which are not concerned with the child.

When fathers are together with the child, it is most often in situations which give immediate rewards - for example, in spontaneous, personal contact with the child in play. On the other hand, however, fathers engage less than the mothers in the routine and time-consuming work that results from having a young child in the house.

The modern father has become the child's playmate and he is, to a greater degree than was the case a few decades ago together with the mother, an important person in the child's socialisation process. With this development, the child has acquired more access to both parents on a more equal level.

Young Children's Social Living Conditions

Planned Children

Today's children come into the world as "planned" children. They are born to parents who have all of the available technical and legal means to decide for themselves if and when they want to have children. It is a reasonable assumption to make, that children born in the Nordic welfare state today, are born to parents who want them and that they arrive more or less on time, as planned.

We no longer believe that children are brought by the stork, or some higher power. We have to bear the responsibility for bringing children into the world.

Children come to us in all innocence; neither as a punishment nor as a gift, but as the result of our own choice. The responsibility is ours - and ours alone. It is the reverse side of the same logic to recognise that a child who comes to us under these circumstances, is granted a number of rights as a birthday present. These rights follow in order to protect the child against the adults' weaknesses, stupidities, and possible second thoughts about what they have brought into the world.

Due to the technical and legal changes introduced, the child and parents face each other as totally new existential subjects.

The Parent-Child Ratio

Another change, that has taken place during the last few decades is that the parents are older, on average, when they have their first child. The average age of the female parent who starts a family in Denmark today is 25.4 years, compared to 22.7 years 20 years ago. Figures from the Nordic countries show similar increases in the age of the male parent.

Another way of looking at this is from the perspective of the birth rate for women over 30. About 12.5% of the women who had their 30th birthday in 1978 were childless. But as many as 25% of those who had their 30th birthday in 1984 were childless.

The demographic prognoses tell us, however, that the great majority of these women will become mothers. In other words, despite the impression gained from the public debate, the proportion of women who remain childless throughout their lives is not increasing. On the contrary, it is falling. 82% of the women in the age range 35-40 live together with at least one child.

20 years ago, 20% of all women reached old age without bearing children. In Denmark, 19.1% of all women born in 1925 had borne no children by the time of their 41st birthday in 1966.

Today, we can count on less than 10% of all women not having had a child before their fertility period is over. 91% of all women born in 1945 in Denmark, gave birth to at least one child by the time they reached their 41st birthday in 1986. That is to say, fewer children are born to more mothers today, than used to be the case.

Motherhood has become more general and more evenly distributed, while the distribution of fatherhood has become more uneven.

In other words, the parent-child ratio has risen. Every child may receive a greater share of its parents' care and attention, all other things being equal.

Siblings

30% of all children in a given year are only children. Many of these children will, of course, have a brother or sister within the next few years. It is estimated that about 80-85% of infants will grow up with at least one sibling, during the period of infancy.

The number of births has fallen abruptly in recent years in virtually all industrialised countries - both capitalist and socialist.

In Denmark, all women of child-bearing age gave birth to a little less than 1 1/2 children on average, in the middle of the 1980's. 20 years ago, the figure was much higher than 2.0 - in other words, what it takes to reproduce the population. The same tendency holds for the other Nordic countries, although the birth rate is on a slightly higher level, especially in Iceland.

The emerging pattern is that it is the third and fourth sibling, in particular, who are not being born. If two siblings are born into the same family, the second child will be born fairly close to the first, so that the period of the adult's life as a parent with infants, is a relatively short and limited one. Only approx. 10% of the children experience a childhood, where they have both older and younger siblings.

Changed Cohabitation Forms

Much fewer children will be born within the framework of a traditional marriage today than before. Marriage popularity today has been declining for some time. For instance, the number of weddings in Denmark fell within the last decade from about 33,000 to under 25,000, to rise again slightly after 1982.

The view of marriage as the "natural" and morally correct framework that children should be born within, has changed in the space of a very short time. In 1965, only about 10% of small Danes and Swedes were born out of wedlock, whereas in 1985 the proportion rose to almost half. This indicates a marked change in norms, a break with centuries' old tradition that legitimate children are born in wedlock and illegimate children are the result of a life of fornication outside the bounds of marriage. Many such couples marry later, while the child is growing up, often with the child as a desirable and accepted participant at the parents wedding.

Whether the parents are married, or just live together as an unmarried couple, does not play an important role for the child in Denmark or Sweden. There is a tendency in these countries towards ranking unmarried, cohabiting couples' relationship, both legally and morally equal with marriage. From the child's point of view, it is important that it lives in a family with two parents and it is of little consequence in daily life whether or not the parents are married.

Children of Divorces

Virtually all newborn children live together with the father and mother. Only about 3% of the children born in Denmark in 1985, were born to single-parent families. Incidentally, this figure has fallen and not - as might be imagined - risen in recent years.

The number of married couples who divorce, has risen abruptly during the last 20-year period:

Figure 3: Divorces per 1,000 married women, 1961/70 and 1984

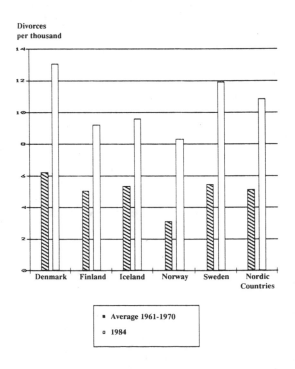

Source: Yearbook of Statistics, 1986, p. 72

For example, in Denmark 14% of the young children growing up to-day have experienced their parents' divorce during the first seven years of their lives. In 1984, 23 out of one thousand 0-2 year-olds and 21 out of one thousand 3-6 year-olds were affected by their parents' divorce.

Children in New Family Constellations

Even in the 1980's, about 80% of children in the Nordic countries between the age range 0 and 6, grow up in a nuclear family (we make no distinction here between parents with/without legal marital status). Out of the total number of children, about three-quarters do, in fact, live with their parents until they reach the age of majority.

In Sweden and Denmark, about 9% of infants (0-6 years) live with a single parent, and 9% of all children of pre-school age live in "combined" family groups (i.e. siblings from different marriages), or two "fused" nuclear families.

A phenomenon which is rather new for some children is growing up with a single mother, or in a so-called "two-nucleus family". Different forms of support from society have made it possible for Nordic children to live in such ways.

Living in a "two-nucleus" family means that the child lives with one of the parents, most often the mother, while at the same time having the opportunity of living with the other parent. Each of the parents will often have formed their own new nuclear family, which the child becomes part of.

Dual Socialisation -
A New Developmental Context for Young Children

An increasing number of young children are cared for outside their home. About 40% of the children in the Nordic countries are cared for by forms of public childcare. In addition, there are a number of privately organised childcare amenities. For example, in Denmark 76% of young children are cared for outside the home, in all, of which 55% are cared for by publicly organised and 21% by privately organised care.

There is a certain variation here, among the Nordic countries. In some countries (Norway, for example) the parents are obliged to find private solutions to their childcare problems. The Nordic country with the greatest number of children in public daycare institutions, is Denmark. Iceland and Norway have fewer (20%). Of the Nordic children, Danish children spend the greatest number of hours daily in daycare institutions (however, no such data are available from Iceland). On average, Danish children spend a couple of hours more weekly in institutions, than children in Finland and Sweden, and 10 hours more than the Norwegian children. Danish children's average daily stay in institutions is 7.2 hours, 5 days per week; a little longer for the 0-2 year-olds than for the 3-6 year-olds.

On the background of these figures, it is evident that a whole generation of small people starts life and lives it in a completely different way to their own parents, when they were children. As the figures show, a very large proportion of the young children in the Nordic countries live in more than one world which will influence their development. One consequence is that it becomes difficult to explain the young child's new reality with such concepts as **primary socialisation** and **secondary socialisation**.

Instead, we prefer to call the situation in which the child finds itself, a "dual-socialisation situation". The child transfers the experience gained in one environment, to the other and vice versa. What happens is, that one of the environments assumes meaning for the child in a way which is dependent on how this element of experience is integrated into the total configuration of experience, in the dual socialisation process.

What is crucial is not what is experienced in the daycare centre itself, but how this fits into the whole life-pattern of experience which the child has. The decisive factors here, are the time-allocation of work that the parents have and the nature of the family structure.

Daycare centres are often very good and stimulating for certain children. But these are often the children who are already doing well in another way. But being at a daycare centre can often be a strain on other children who are having a bad time of it already. Somewhere or other in the gospel of St. Matthew it says, "unto everyone that hath shall be given".

A dual-socialisation analysis can help us capture the "St. Matthew effect", in the socialisation process of modern childhood.

Dual Socialisation - Self Control and Intimacy

What is it about social development in its headlong dash into the postmodern age, which has specific effects upon children's lives within the family?

In this connection, we would like to draw attention to a social process, the civilising process. The analysis of this process is based on the sociologist Norbert Elias' (1978) theory. According to Elias, one of the characteristics of this process is the greater demands made on us to perform in an increasing number of public arenas.

From this, it follows that people have learnt to control their feelings and exercise restraint in all kinds of situations. One must learn to act circumspectly in the public arena, so that one can be in the company of women, for example, without attacking them sexually; or make a point with a debating opponent without losing one's temper and punching him, etc. One of the results of this civilising process means getting a grip on one's emotions and keeping them under social control. According to Elias, this development in the direction of an increasing **ability to exercise inner self-control,** has been going on for centuries in the West and is still going on. Children now seem to learn this control at a very early age. When still toddlers at the daycare centre, they make their appearance in the public arena, where it is just this ability of self-control which is considered to be a sign of adaptability.

Daycare centres are public environments; public institutions, one might say. Meeting people in such environments has its own dynamic, which is quite different from the dynamic going on in more familial situations. In private life, people's interactions are governed, to a large extent, by the individuals concerned.

In public life, it is the dispassionate behaviour which is uppermost, while the affective aspects of the interaction are kept in check. The interaction has become "instrumental". In the public arena, people's conduct is usually regulated by unwritten rules enforcing "civilised" behaviour. These cultural observations come to life when one studies the interaction of children in the Nordic day-nurseries and within their families.

In spite of what many people might think, there is relatively less display of emotion in the everyday life of the day-nursery "dayroom", than in the family. How children relate to the staff and vice-versa, is instrumental to a very large extent. On the whole, children show an exceptional ability to exercise control over their impulses and hold back any display of emotion. Their conduct is already "civilised" at a very early stage of their childhood.

Perhaps this is precisely what the disguised function of the daycare centre is: to "civilise" the children at an already tender age, thereby facilitating the course of social development?

How does this affect the children's lives within the family? one might ask. In the private sphere and from the child's point of view, it is the parents who play the parts of co-actors. The child sends out a whole range of emotions in their directions: frustration, aggression, a craving for love and affection, and the need for a good cuddle. But perhaps none of this has been visible during the day, at the daycare centre.

The professional pedagogues are usually friendly, but keep a distance between themselves and the children. They are the instruments for implementing the correct rules of behaviour in the public arena.

The specific function of the parents in their relation to the child, is rather to respond to the child's emotional outbursts, and manifest an equivalent show of feelings. At this point, we can grasp what is one of the most important functions of the modern family: **the family as an intimacy sanctuary**.

Young Children's Cultural Living Conditions

Norm-pluralism in Changing Societies

An important feature of Nordic children's cultural condition is the increasing rate of change in the Nordic societies; innovation and adjustment to new technology and other forms of production and marketing, make new demands on man's qualification. It is not only the demands for new knowledge that are prominent, but the need for other psychological properties also changes along with societal development. For example, demands related to modern management style are completely different to those related to earlier styles. Now, properties such as the ability to cooperate in small social groups, are also expected. But what about the future? Demands for psychological competence today can become obsolescent on the other side of the turn of the millennium, when our children have grown up. In other words, traditional ways of upbringing might soon become outdated - even though they are modern now. History can supply us with many examples of how upbringers' requirements as to how children should and must behave, have changed markedly through the times. It is actually not more than one generation ago that obedience, orthodoxy, and fear of God were the bearing elements and good commendable pedagogy. At the same time, the punishment for disobedience, a good beating, was an acceptable means by which to raise a new generation. But even with a degree of understatement, this can hardly be said to be the mainstay of today's view of upbringing.

As a result of the loss of norm-stability, the individual, the small group and society must attempt to build up new norms and values which can replace those no longer in operation. At this point in time, we are in the position where norm-pluralism is established as a principle in modern society. We must live with the fact that there are many, often contradictory ways in which life can be composed and that it is now very much up to the individual alone, or together with others, to define the meaning of life.

Norm-pluralism also involves that the relations among generations become complicated. Modern parents cannot immediately apply and accept their own mothers' and fathers' way of upbringing, since these belong to another time. As new parents, it is necessary for them to "create upbringing" again without unambiguous and clear help from others. As a new parent, one must face the fact that one will only function as a model for one's child to a very limited degree. Also, in extension of this, one must face the fact that parents - as the product of their own upbringing in bygone days - must socialise their children here and now, so that they may function in a future that not even they know about. This is not only the fundamental condition for new parents, but for everyone who is concerned with children's growing up, care, and upbringing in our society.

A consequence of this is that parents today listen eagerly to the experts' advice discover that they often change their minds and prove themselves to be unreliable. Nobody can give hard and fast advice; the know-how changes just as quickly as the development itself. Uncertainty has become almost chronic. Different phenomena, it seems, spring up in the wake of the uncertainty:

- A double tendency which calls for both commitment and the abdication of responsibility with regard to children's upbringing. Parents appear to be more sensitive about their children's needs and wants, than ever before and are quite prepared to meet them. But they are less and less certain as to how they should accomplish this. The result is a combination of commitment to the child and an abdication from the job of actually bringing the child up which, instead, has become more and more the province of the expert.

- An increasing professionalisation of the supervision of the child. This has increasingly become a question of educated personnel being paid to give a helping hand as the child grows up. Up-bringing engages all of the skills of the pedagogic artificer - rather than the transfer of fixed values and outlook on life.

- A -"pedagogicisation" of the child's life and of the environment it grows up in. One of the things this involves is making sure that the activities that the child is engaged in, are suitably "stimulating" and development-oriented - though nobody quite knows for what exactly.

- A "pathologisation" of the undesirable features in what, in itself, is a quite normal behavioural repertoire. "Normal behaviour" is defined more strictly than ever, according to the way the functional requisites of institutions, changes in the environment, and "time-structuring", impinge upon it. Such requisites often lie behind the pedagogic and psychological insights, upon which the foundations for childcare are laid. One example of a child not living up to the functional requisites, is when the staff feel that it is too "noisy" - at least from their own point of view. Another example would be, when a child shows a tendency to isolate itself from the hurly-burly situation it is confronted with at the day-nursery. These are the times when they call on the special services of trained pedagogs, psychologists, or experts in remedial therapy. It is their job to define the undesirable behavioural traits of the child as symptoms of one kind of dysfunction or another, on the part of the child itself. Actually, even the criteria of normality are undergoing a process of adjustment, to conform to a more and more rigidly defined bureaucratic model of children's behaviour. The "real" behind-the-scenes ideal, is the properly functioning child - as seen from the point of view of "child administration".

Socialization of Young Children in the Nordic Countries

Children's Growing Independence in Relation to the Family

In the Nordic countries, we see a tendency to regard children and parents as independent subjects, with separate legal status. In Sweden for example, a recent government report gave serious consideration to granting children the rights of separation from their parents, and awarding them the status of a legal party in separation proceedings. The State provides maintenance benefits and legal assistance to children, and legislates on the relationship between children and parents. Examples of this would be the law adopted in Sweden and Norway against corporal punishment and the obligation placed on parents to see that the child is properly stimulated and receives an education consistent with its aptitudes.

The State can also intervene in the life of the family when its representatives - such as nurses, pedagogues, teachers, etc. - have found that there is something wrong with the child-parent relationship. Assistance can be provided through the mobilisation of the social services; strong pressure can be placed on parents to live up to certain obligations, or the necessary steps can be taken to remove the child from the care of the parents. The number of interventions of this type has been on the increase during the last few years.

When parents feel that circumstances are such that they cannot manage to give their children all of the personal care they need, they may appeal to the State, which is statutorily required to look after all children in need of welfare assistance.

Today, it is also possible for children to appeal directly to the State, without having to use their parents as intermediaries. In Norway, for example, children are entitled to the assistance of the State against their parents, by appealing to a special "Children's ombudsmand".

When family-sociologists talk about the family's function in society, we usually see it as a two-sided relationship. The children are seen as part of a family, with the parents as their spokemen. But this model is gradually being superseded by a new development.

Triangle relation: state - children - parents

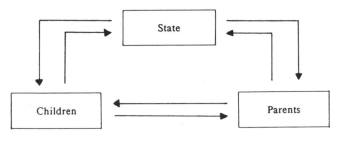

Fig. 4

The stage is set for a new "eternal triangle", which means that the State can intervene more directly in the relationship to children, as both a supportive and a controlling instance. On the other hand, the children are given better opportunities, via various channels, to appeal directly to the State. In the Nordic welfare states, therefore, the evaluation of the child's rights is no longer exclusively subject to the parents' sovereign rule.

The Relationship Between Parents and Children in Legislation[1]

Nordic law today, still builds upon the premise that the child must be cared for and brought up in the family. The parents have a duty to provide for the child, to care for it and take decisions about the child's conditions. However, it can be interesting to consider the degree to which the legislative power attempts to instruct the parents, as to how the child must be provided for and brought up. Marked differences among the Nordic countries become apparent here. These differences also reveal interesting cultural and ideological differences among the countries.

There are, of course, limits for the fixed norms that society can set for the child's provision, since it is the parents who must bear the expense. In this connection, it is even more important that parents'

---

[1] We wish to thank assistant professor Nina von Hielmcrone for the preparation of this section.

conditions in society differ a great deal with respect to job, housing, and cultural conditions. In Danish law, this is expressed in the elastic formulation of The Laws on Children's Legal Status - paragraph 13, subsection 1: "The child must be provided for, brought up and educated with due consideration as to the parents' living conditions and the child's best interests." The State may only intervene and if the situation demands it, give the parents more precise suggestions and instructions with respect to their provision and upbringing of the child, in cases where the child is neglected to such a degree that the social assistance law's rules concerning children and youths, become relevant. Consequently, the State also covers the expenses related to these suggestions and injunctions.

There could be said to be consistency in an approach of this kind to the relationship between children and their parents: In that one entrusts the child's parents with the duties and the responsibilities, one must also give them reasonably broad freedom of action.

On the other hand, society is also concerned that the conditions that the child lives under are reasonably secure, both materially and socially. The modern family in the Nordic countries is no more private than that the public service can intervene. The question is, how can one ensure that the child thrives, on the one hand, and avoid intervening too much in the parent/child relationship, on the other. As we shall see in this section, there are interesting differences among the Nordic countries, as to the evaluation of how the public instances manifest themselves in relation to the family.

In the case of Danish law, society's attitude is expressed thus: On the one hand, one leaves the main part of the responsibility to the parents while giving them a certain degree of economic support in the form of family allowance, rent rebate, help to offset childcare expenses, etc, on the other hand. In addition, social offices can extend support in those situations where it is considered that the child's well-being is threatened. Furthermore, as the most extreme consequence, the state can instigate forced removal of the child from its parents.

In other Nordic countries, such as Finland, Norway, and to a certain extent, Sweden, for example, it has been decided in civil legislation, i.e. the rules which directly regulate the relationship between children and their parents, to weight more "moral" instructions as to the child's upbringing, than is the case in Denmark. When Denmark was about to effect the changes in the custody laws which came into effect from 1st January, 1986, and introduced the possibility for unmarried and separated/divorced parents of shared child-custody, there was a great deal of discussion as to whether Denmark should follow the other Nordic countries' example by telling parents how to bring their children up. The same discussion had also been carried on earlier, in connection with the question of whether to repeal the right to inflict corporal punishment. It was concluded that Denmark - contrary to what is the case in the family legislation of the other Nordic countries - would avoid, as far as possible, making stipulations which might be characterised as effecting parents' attitude to upbringing. However, the legislative body chose to extend the stipulations concerning the content of child custody to include a duty to protect the child from physical and mental cruelty.

In this respect, the attitudes of the other Nordic countries have been somewhat different. For example, in the Norwegian and Finnish rules, there are direct instructions as to the child's right to be consulted. Furthermore, the parents are instructed to support the child in becoming - and to encourage it to become - an independent and responsible individual. Also, the child must receive an education which is consistent with its abilities and wishes. The stipulations are not sanctioned, however. That is to say, parents are not punished for transgressing them. Furthermore, the stipulations almost appear to be an expression of the state's attempt to effect parents' attitudes.

The Danish legal conception is also characteristic on another point, as compared to Finnish and Norwegian law. This concerns the conception of the degree to which a fixing of more exact rules for the inclusion of public authorities in conflicts between children and parents, can actually contribute to a genuine solution of the problems.

If we look at the rules concerning child custody and visiting rights, we see in Finnish and Norwegian law in particular that the courts have very extensive powers to take decisions about the child's conditions. This can - and does - have extreme consequences with respect to the implicated children's social conditions. There is, of course, a certain consistency on the part of society in this, when law concurrently gives general attitude forming guidelines for the child's upbringing.

The most extensive are the Finnish rules, which decisively enable the public services to regulate the child's social relations to those nearest and dearest to it. A Finnish judge can take custody of the child from the father and mother and give it to others. Alternatively, he can appoint "parallel parents", i.e. persons who have custody of the child along with the parents. As a starting point, Finnish parents can - as in the other Nordic countries - agree upon shared custody, or that one of them is to have custody of the child. Also, they can decide together where the child is to live, etc. However, if the parents cannot reach an agreement, or if the judge finds that there are good grounds for doing so, he can overrule the parents' agreement. Contrary to for examole Danish tradition, he can even take decisions in regard to details of the child's conditions. For example, which obligations the individual custody holder must fulfil. He can also charge the father and mother with the joint custody of the child - even against their wishes and even if they have reached another agreement between themselves.

The Norwegian rules give the courts more extensive powers with regard to intervention in the regulation of the child's social conditions, than is the case in Denmark. For example, a Norwegian judge can decide which of the parents the child is to live with. According to Norwegian law, this entails a curtailment of the other parent's right to make decisions for the child, because the parent with whom the child does not live cannot oppose the child being moved to another town. Neither can he/she interfere in the day-to-day upbringing of the child, if the public authorities, through the judge, have so decided. In Sweden, it is also possible to take custody away from both of the child's parents and to award it to other adults. In all other respects, however, the Swedish rules are like the Danish.

Cultural differences also manifest themselves with regard to visiting rights. Since the concrete form of the visiting rights is so decisive in the structuring of Nordic children's social conditions, then the children in the cultures are also given different conditions. In Sweden and Norway, for example, it is possible to award visiting rights to other people than the parents against the parents' wishes. They can be awarded to grandparents or to one of the parent's earlier common law husband or wife. In Norway, however, this is only the case if one of the parents is dead. That is to say, this constitutes an attempt to effect a kind of "replacement" for lost relations.

Rules about shared child custody were introduced in Denmark in 1986. But it is interesting to see again that the attitudes implicit in the rules are marked by reticence. The rules constitute an attempt to encourage the parents to reach an agreement on the questions of shared custody of the child and the sharing of time together with it. Furthermore, the parents are offered the support and advice of a child expert, to help them to clarify whether they can make such agreements.

In Denmark, then, one has refrained from making rules that give the judge, or the state administrative body in any district the power to charge parents with shared child custody. This can only be established on the basis of an agreement, if the parents are not married. Also, any one of the parents can annul the agreement at any time. In Denmark, only the parents can hold shared custody of a child and it is also a precondition of their doing so, that they have reached agreement on all of the important questions related to the child's upbringing. It is not possible, as it is in Norway, to get the authorities to determine where the child is to live, for example. If Danish parents cannot agree, then the only solution is the annulment of the shared custody of the child. One can only acquire the authorities' support in connection with visiting rights; in this case, the authorities concerned would be the state administrative body in the district in question, or the bailiff. But visiting rights cannot be awarded as long as there exists shared child custody. Once again, we see that Danish practice attaches great importance to getting the father and mother to reach an agreement.

Only the parents can acquire visiting rights in Denmark. However, the following question has been discussed: Should one give the possibility of being awarded visiting rights to other persons whom the child has close ties to, as is, for example, the case in Sweden. For example, a situation in which a previous common law husband or wife is awarded visiting rights with the child, against the wishes of a parent. Converted into practice, which is at variance with Norwegian or Finnish practice, for example, it must also create different social conditions for young children in the North.

Superordinately, it can thus be concluded with respect to the legal regulation of young children's social conditions, that there exist both interesting cultural similarities and differences:

-   It applies to all the Nordic countries that parents must provide for their children, take the responsibility for their care and take decisions on their behalf. Even in modern Nordic childhood, with a pronounced degree of upbringing taking place out of the parents' and the family's reach, it is still the parents' responsibility in the Nordic societies in the 80's.

    In some cases, the authorities only intervene when it is apparent that these responsibilities are not lived up to.
-   But there are important cultural differences, especially between Finland and Norway, on one hand, and Denmark and Sweden, on the other, with consequences for the state's regulation of the child's social living conditions. In Finland, the state cannot only undertake an extensive and active attitude-forming role in relation to the child's parents. It must also strengthen this role further through detailed regulation of the child's social conditions - even in spite of the parents' wishes.

    This also applies, by and large, to Norway. In this respect, Sweden lies somewhere between Denmark and the other countries.

In conclusion we ascertain that an unambiguous and clear marking of the parents' and the family's responsibility for a new generation of children is prevailing in the modern Nordic societies. This in spite of the fact that we live in a time where the public authorities intervene in many and various ways and form our children's living conditions. The clearest example of this is probably the fact that, even though the father and mother are charged with the main responsibility for the child's thriving and development, they have no control or direct influence on the way in which the child develops in the childcare within the public sphere.

In precisely this area there are such clear differences among the Nordic countries in the presentation of the rules, despite the similarities in development that otherwise exist among the countries.

Societal Development in Relation to Young Children in Contemporary Nordic countries - An Overview

Here, the most central societal changes must be summarised in a series of points, from the perspective of their consequences for childhood:

1. **Urbanisation**

    During this century, the increasing immigration in the cities has formed modern childhood as a so-called "urban childhood", along with the physical and social conditions that are its consequences. After the second world war, this has taken place very quickly in Finland and Iceland. Because of the fast migration from country to city, one can speak of an extensive "cultural lag" in these countries. Parents' and grandparents' experiences in the rural way of life will not harmonise with their children's condition of growing up in the urban living environment. The city and its life have thus become the physical and social life-space of an increasing number of young Nordic children, where they live their daily lives today. By far the majority of Nordic children today (over 80%) grow up in urban environments.

2. **Changes in the Population Composition**

    The number of children in the North has fallen and this will have consequences that will reach into the next century. Children are a living and vital part of our everyday lives, but the proportion of the Nordic population that the children now represent has fallen to about 8%. For example, there are about 380,000 young children in Denmark today, but within just a decade, the number has fallen by 100,000. With respect to young children as a proportion of the total population, Denmark has reached an all time Nordic low. In Denmark today, the very young (0-6 year-olds) represent only 7.7% of the total population, whereas Iceland has the highest percentage with 12.5%.

At the same time the "young child period" in the adults' lives has become an episode that one recovers from relatively quickly. It is not the same as for earlier generations; a more or less permanent condition in the adults' lives. One of the reasons for this is not only that fewer children are born, but also that the few who are, are born in close succession.

Even an increase in the birthrate in the foreseeable future will not be able to compensate for the fall in the birthrate in the last decades. The consequences are not only that society becomes poorer in children, but also that the children when they become productive adults, will constitute the smaller part of society that will have to provide for an increasing number of elderly.

3. Changes in Working Conditions

The degree to which new technology changes work processes and demands the ability to adjust, is increasing. This is also the case with parents. Demands for new norms arise in accordance with a new future - and to a new generation. However, because of society's innovation process, our perspective of the future as a point of orientation and a guideline for the formation of norms, is becoming unclear. This gives rise to a double-sidedness in the socialisation of children: On the one hand we know that we do not know what future we must suite them for.

The Arisal of The New Middle Class: Due to the education explosion in the 60's and the development of the social state, a new ideological direction has become apparent in society. Researchers, experts, professional upbringers and other people who work directly or indirectly with children, now influence the child-ideological climate in the North, more than ever before. This new classes power is not derived from the disposition of economic capital, but plays an important role, on the other hand, through its access to and control of a "cultural capital" in society.

To a very high degree young children's lives are influenced by the particular socio-economic conditions that the child grows up under: Young children in the North, then, still live in different ideological spaces depending on the parents' socio-economic position in society. Therefore, children are effected in their early upbringing environment in the family, by those attitudes and that particular way of life of which their parents are the bearers.

The woman and the mother of young children have gained access to the labour market. This fact, which will not change considerably in the years to come, has created what may be modern childhood's most obvious change: Institutionalisation with its most marked consequences for a new generation of children.

4. **Increased Prosperity - But Also Modern Poverty**

We note that in general, young children's material standard of living is said to have improved over the last few decades. This concerns the economy and manifests itself in an improved housing standard, as well as a disposition over many material amenities. This applies especially to the prototypical family with young children, where both parents work and have 1 or 2 children.

On the other hand, it must also be stressed that for a minority, actual economical problems are still a reality in the North, in the 80's. A marked accumulation of such economical problems is to be found within the group of single breadwinners, i.e. single women with children.

5. **Changes in the Family Pattern**

Smaller families: Modern childhood entails growing up in a smaller sibling group, with all of its attendant consequences for social development. Today, most children have only one sibling. More children are only children today, than was the case in the 60's.

More divorces: More children experience divorce and more live with only one parent today, due to divorce. However, despite this, by far the majority of young children in the Nordic countries in the 80's, still live with both of their biological parents.

More children today live in "Two nucleus families", i.e., in social constellations where they alternately live with the mother in her new family and the father in his new family.

New Ways of Living Together: Unmarried cohabitation reflects another, more relaxed attitude to marriage and having children out of wedlock. This has not replaced marriage. However, during the last decades it is a form of living together which many children have been born into and which has been the frame within which they live their lives.

6. Increased Public Engagement in Childcare

Institutionalisation is a distinctive feature of modern childhood. Through the last quarter century and for many years to come, young children (and older children) have spent and will spend time within the public socialisation spheres. The resulting dual-socialisation means not only that the children are looked after by others than their parents, but that the new childhood is formed in another way - on the one hand, by the family's set of norms and upbringing practice, and on the other by the professional upbringers' set of norms and upbringing practice.

7. The Cultural and Ideological Changes in Childhood

The "supraculture" has an increasingly greater influence on children's daily lives. By this, we mean that TV, books and toys, among other things of which children are consumers, are being internationalised. Specifically national-cultural products for children are gradually coming to enjoy only a marginal existence and will be severely exposed to the culturel homogenisation that is taking place everywhere in the post-modern technology and media societies.

Humanisation: An analysis of a.o. legislation and its view of children reveals the fact that increased consideration is shown for the concept of the child as an individual with its own interests and needs. The child is perceived ideologically by the Nordic societies today, as a being whose interests and living conditions must be protected. Even, in some cases, if this is contrary to the parent's wishes. Conversely, in other areas, society demonstrates the giving of a lower priority to consideration of the child. The working hours, traffic conditions, the physical layout of housing areas and the lack of opportunity for parents to look after their sick children in some of the countries, are to young children's parents just some examples which indicate modern society's lack of consideration of children's conditions.

Norm-pluralism as socialisation's fundamental condition, is becoming a superordinate, common condition for all upbringers. Due to the rate of change in society, the norms that every upbringing must build upon also become fluid and relative. We live in a time which, on the one hand, opens up for enormous, new possibilities in the socialisation of children, but on the other, for a diffuse and unclear situation which is a common, shared condition that no one can transcend. Perplexity, confusion and dependence on experts in questions of upbringing, are possible consequences. As such, these fundamental ambiguities in socialisation are not completely new, but are of far more pronounced importance now than previously. The reason for this is that the societal process creating the modern change in norms and their diffuseness is accelerating faster than ever. This is also a vital part of children's cultural living conditions today.

References and sources

Andenæs, A. & Haavind, H. (1987). *Små barns livsvilkår i Norge.* (Young children's living conditions in Norway). Oslo: Universitetsforlaget.

Ariès, P. (1962). *Centuries of childhood.* New York: Vintage.

Christoffersen, M. N. (1987). *Familien under forandring?* (The changing family). København: Socialforskningsinstituttet.

Christoffersen, M. N. et al. (1987). *Hvem passer vore børn?* (Who takes care of our children?). København: Socialforskningsinstituttet.

Dencik, L. (1987). *Opvækst i postmodernismen.* (Growing up in the post-modern age). In P. S. Jørgensen (Ed.) *Børn i nye familiemønstre.* (Children in new family constellations). København: Hans Reitzels Forlag.

Elias, N. (1987). *Über den Prozess der Zivilization.* (On the civilizing process). Frankfurt a.M.: Suhrkamp Verlag (1939).

KRON-projektet. (1987). *Barnomsorg i Norden.* (Childcare in the Nordic countries). Stockholm: Statskontoret.

Lahikainen, A.-R. & Strandell, H. (1988). *Lapsen kasvuehdot Suomessa.* (Young children's living conditions in Finland). Helsinki: Gaudeamus.

Langsted, O. & Sommer, D. (1988). *Småbørns livsvilkår i Danmark.* (Young children's living conditions in Denmark). København: Hans Reitzels Forlag.

Postman, N. (1984). *The disappearance of childhood.* New York: Delacorte Press.

Shorter, E. (1975). *The making of the modern family.* New York: Basic Books.

Social Security in the Nordic countries. (1984). Helsinki: Nordic Statistical Secretariat.

Yearbook of Nordic Statistics 1984 and 1986. (1985, and 1987). Stockholm and Copenhagen: Nordic Council and Nordic Statistical Secretariat.

PART II

DANISH BIBLIOGRAPHY

YOUNG CHILDREN'S MATERIAL CONDITIONS

Berthelsen, O. (1985). *De faldende fødselstal: årsager - konsekvenser* /The Declining Birthrate: Reasons - Consequences. København: Socialforskningsinstituttet, pjece, 14. ISBN: 87-7487-264-8. In Danish.

Summary: A study of the declining birthrate in Denmark and an estimation of the consequences for the future.

Theoretical frame of reference: Not explicitly expressed, but the preparation indicates a sociological frame of reference directed by empirical facts.

Method employed: The latest statistical data pertaining to birthrate.

Results: The study concludes that the birthrate in Denmark has been declining for many years, as it has in the industrialised countries as a whole. We are now in a situation, where the population is slowly being reduced because of the declining birthrate and declining immigration in relation to mortality and emigration. Consequences for the future are outlined.

* * *

Berthelsen, O. (1980). *Den unge familie i 70'erne*/The Young Family in the 70ies. København: Teknisk forlag. ISBN: 87-7487-175-7. In Danish. With an English summary.

Summary: A survey of the conditions of starting a family in Denmark in 1975; young families' housing conditions, women's employment outside the home and the sharing of housework.

Theoretical frame of reference: Not explicitly expressed, but the preparation indicates a sociological, family-theoretical frame of reference. A strongly empirically directed work.

1 (Part II)

Method employed: Interviews with a randomly selected, nationally representative sample of 5.420 women aged 18-49. A statistical preparation.

Results: Establishing the family: Cohabitation union is an initial phase before the children arrive and occurs typically in families with infants. Usually the first child is born out of wedlock. Housing: The family with children has the highest expenses and has relatively larger and better housing than the population in general. Women's employment conditions: 71% in 1975. 2/3 want part-time work, while the children are young. Housework: The husband assists more in 1975 than in 1964, but there is not an equal division of labour. The husband participates more actively in the young families. However, it is conceivable, that the traditional sex roles will be adopted, when the first child is born. The extent of women's employment outside the home has no connection with the husband's participation in housework.

* * *

Børnefamiliernes *økonomi og arbejdsforhold*/The Economy and Working Conditions of Families with Children. København: Børnekommissionen, udvalgsrapport, 1. ISBN 87-503-3264-3. In Danish.

Summary: Describes the development in family-political legislation from 1964 until approximately 1980 and discusses the living conditions of families with children in areas such as: labour-market, income, consumption, housing and use of daycare arrangements. Special groups, such as single breadwinners, large families, low-income families and so on, are described. The consequences of the existing apportionment of resources policies are also described and the committee's recommendations with respect to the family with children in relation to these areas, are presented.

Theoretical frame of reference: Not explicitly expressed, but within an interdisciplinary sociological frame of reference.

Method employed: Analysis of existing research and statistical material. With no empirical material of its own.

Results: Some families do not have the resources for securing reasonable conditions for their children. The family with children has a lower income per individual than the family without children. The committee suggests, among other things, a reduction in working hours for parents with 0-8 year-old children and presents, in general, a number of suggestions with regard to labour-market policy, economic benefits, daycare arrangements for children and housing policy.

* * *

Småbørn *i bolig og miljø*/Young Children's Housing and Environment. København: Børnekommissionen. Særtryk af udvalgsrapport, 2. ISBN 87-503-3303-8. In Danish.

Summary: An analysis of and suggestions for improvements in young children's living conditions in neighbourhood environments, family housing and micro- and macro environments (one of the few analyses of young children and physical environments in Denmark).

Theoretical frame of reference: Not explicitly expressed. An explanatory work within an interdisciplinary sociological frame of reference.

Method employed: An analysis of existing research and material, with no empirical material of its own.

Results: The family with young children has good housing in a traditional sense. There were great differences in young children's housing conditions, and the distribution follows, by and large, the distribution of social groups. The relatively high standard of family housing, however, is connected with high expenses, which lie heavily on the economy of the family with young children. Traffic is a risk factor for young children in many housing areas. There is a high accident rate, especially for 3-6 year-old children and limitations in young children's opportunities for self-expression. The housing areas are often physically alike, socially one-sided and not conductive to fantasy and play. Parents of young children often lack the political potency to alter this. The committee suggests: Facilitation of the establishment situation of families with young children, support of low-income families housing, promotion of urban renewal, improvement of pedagogical amenities, physical amenities for play and unfolding, better traffic environments, desegregation, the guarding of young children's interests when building new housing areas, creation of a change of attitude in adults, ensuring more time for the families to be together at home and in the neighbourhood environment and promotion of a local community model.

* * *

Schultz Jørgensen, P. (1978). *Forbrugsfamilien og dens børn*/The Consumer Family and its Children. København: Akademisk forlag. ISBN 87-500-1578-8. In Danish.

Summary: An analysis of the nuclear family's historical and modern conditions of existence and consequences regarding its internal structure of social roles and social relations.

Theoretical frame of reference: Sociological and social-psychological, without being characterised by a particular "school".

Method employed: Theoretical method, with no empirical material of its own. Illustrates conditions in Denmark, especially on the basis of American surveys.

Results: The nuclear family is a historical and social structure. Its modern form as a unit of consumption and as an emotional stronghold will be of decisive importance for the quality or lack of quality of the parent-child relationship.

* * *

Søndergård Kristensen, T. (1978). *Kvinders arbejdsmiljø*/Women's Working Environment. København: Fagbevægelsens Forskningsråd. ISBN 87-557-0967-2. In Danish.

Summary: Study of health-, work- and family relations of employees in 7 women's trades in Denmark.

Theoretical frame of reference: Not explicitly expressed, but a sociological approach directed by importance attached to the empirical side.

Method employed: A questionnaire survey from 1976-1977 including 3.139 answers. The preparation is statistical and quantitative.

Results: Many of the women are primarily motivated to work by the salary. Because of the economic circumstances, there is no real choice between home and work. The distribution of housework in the home is typically traditional. Men and women do not agree on the degree to which it is shared, but generally it is the women who have the main responsibility and most of the work. They even look after sick children, also in families where the woman earns most of the money. Families with young children use day-care, family, neighbours and others relatively more than families with bigger children, who to a higher degree attend kindergarten.

* * *

Gøtzsche, V. (1984). *Som forældre vi dele? At være to om barn og hjem*/As Parents We Share? Sharing the Responsibility for Looking After the Child at Home. København: Gyldendal. ISBN 87-00-54754-9. In Danish.

Summary: A study of the everyday life of Danish families with young children and their division of labour regarding home and children. Analysis of the concrete division of labour and deeper psychological interpretation of the barriers against division of labour.

Theoretical frame of reference: Not explicitly expressed, but within a sociological frame of reference with the main emphasis on a therapeutical psychological analysis.

Method employed: Combined quantitative and qualitative analysis. Questionnaire of 471 fathers and mothers, and interviews with 15 couples with children in 1980.

Results: The division of labour between parents with young children is unequal. The women do most of the housework and the child-minding. The deeper reasons for this is not only the man's reluctance, but also the resistance of the woman against giving up the role as "the good and indispensable mother". Furthermore, men's and women's different thresholds with regard to when and how a household chore is to be done, plays a role. Thus, the family's "common" areas of responsibility are experienced very differently in relation to sex.

* * *

Storace, K. et al. (1982). *Småbørns vilkår i lokalsamfundet belyst ud fra familiens situation*/Infants' Conditions in the Local Community, Illustrated on the Basis of the Family's Situation. 2.udg. Farum: Farum kommune, Farum. Forskningsgruppen: Børns opvækst i Farum. Områdeanalyse, 1. ISBN 87-88097-05-6. In Danish.

Summary: A project aimed at gaining more exact knowledge about the growth of young children in a specific municipality, especially with reference to the consequences of institutionalisation and the physical division of the local community in proportion to the family.

Theoretical frame of reference: Sociological and social-psychological interdisciplinary models with the main emphasis on the process of socialisation.

Method employed: Questionnaire survey of 312 adults as well as interviews with parents with young children. The preparation is quantitative and statistical.

Results: Work-time versus time spent with the family: The families experience a dilemma between participation in the social production and the responsibility for the socialisation of the 0-6 year-olds, which the parents feel is their main responsibility. Family housing: The family with young children in Farum live, as a rule, in larger accommodation built after 1960. 50% of the families are new arrivals from between 1970-75. The connection with the nearby environment is relatively loose. Play conditions: 2/3 of the parents are not satisfied with the play facilities for their children. 1/5 of the tenants find, that the play facilities are good as compared to 50% of those, who own their houses. Traffic: 2/3 find, that the traffic is either "very" dangerous or "less" dangerous. Playmates: 50% of the children have, according to the parents, too few, or none at all living near the home. Only 18% of the children have access to a playground. There is a shortage of good playgrounds near the home. Neighbourhood: 1/3 of the families with young children have no contact with the neighbours. Single parents with full-time employment have the least contact with their neighbours. 50% have daily contact with their neighbours, or during the week, both practically and socially. Municipal offers and arrangements for support: 72% of the 0-6 year-old children are taken care of in daycare centres, 11% in the home and 6% by family or others. 2/3 prefer that the children are taken care of half-time in a centre.

* * *

Småbørn *og tidlig indsats*/Young Children and Early Intervention. (1980). København: Børnekommissionen. Udvalgsrapport, 4. ISBN 87-503-3270-8. In Danish.

Summary: An analysis of a suggestion of early intervention regarding young children and their parents.

Theoretical frame of reference: Not explicitly expressed, but a sociologically open approach.

Method employed: An analysis of existing research and available material. Clarification with no empirical material of its own.

Results: The community of today is divided between the parents' working-life and the children's institutional life, where they only meet at the beginning and at the end of the day. The committee suggests: Longer holidays and more spare-time for parents with young children, a strengthening of the childcare policy, information on children's and parents' needs, better family guidance, better care and family facilities for the child during illness, a more family-minded birth situation, strengthening of the health visitor function, and a general improvement to increase the effectivity of the public system with regard to the newly established family, is discussed.

* * *

YOUNG CHILDREN'S SOCIAL CONDITIONS

Berthelsen, O. & P. Linde (1985). *Efterspørgsel efter offentlig dag-pasning*/The Demand for Public Daycare. København: Socialforsk-ningsinstituttet. Publikation, 141. ISSN 0583-712x. In Danish.

Summary: A study of the factors that create the demand for public daycare, illustrated on the basis of the family's life together, economy, family housing and the number of children living at home.

Theoretical frame of reference: Not explicitly expressed, but a strongly directed empirical sociological approach.

Method employed: Representative interviews conducted in 1975, re-gister information from 1981 and data from smaller interviews conducted in 1983. Quantitative/statistical adaptations and a small qualitative analysis.

Results: If the mother is working outside the home, is an employee, is a single breadwinner and has a child, she has need of public daycare. The demand is not met by the public supply, which is too small. Mothers give outside employment high priority and demand security, continuity and more flexible arrangements of public daycare.

* * *

Bøgh, C. & P. Schultz Jørgensen (red.). (1985). *Småbørn - familie - samfund*/Young Children - Family - Society. København: Hans Reit-zels Forlag. ISBN 87-412-3855-9. In Danish.

Summary: A relatively varied selection of Danish research on young children 1980-1985, within the fields of "newborn children and their local environment", "the development of young children", "daycare centres and family daycare", "sick children" and "lack of childminding". These are not all equally relevant.

Theoretical frame of reference: Very pluralistic, dependent on the individual author. Outlines a future of Danish research on young children in the 1980s as being far from theoretically homogeneous.

Method employed: Quantitative with large samples and questionnaires and small qualitative projects. The latter project type is predominant.

* * *

Christensen, E. (1980). *Første barn: sociale og psykiske ændringer for kvinden, manden og parret /* The First Child: Social and Psychological Changes for the Woman, the Man and the Couple. Hellerup: Dansk Psykologisk Forlag. ISBN 87-87580-31-4. In Danish.

Summary: A study of the social and psychological consequences in Denmark in the 1970s of having the first child.

Theoretical frame of reference: Marxist existentialism. Extended theory as a basis for interpretation.

Method employed: Qualitative, in depth interviews and questionnaires with 38 women and 38 men in 1975-76. Both quantitative and qualitative preparation.

Results: The transition from being a couple to being a family is indeed problematic for parents, who do not want to settle into the traditional sex roles. These sex roles create inequality in the relationship to the child and in the internal role distribution in the family. There is a decline in social contacts after a family is established. Generally speaking, family establishment is a difficult transition for adults.

* * *

Diderichsen, B. (1976). *Den 0-3 årige samfundsborger*/The 0-3 Year-Old Member of Society. København: Hans Reitzels Forlag. ISBN 87-412-3100-7. In Danish.

Summary: An analysis of the importance of the social conditions for the young child, directly and indirectly, mediated through the parents and the daycare centre.

Theoretical frame of reference: Of a Marxist orientation within sociology and social psychology with the involvement of psychoanalytical psychology.

Method employed: A theoretical analysis of everyday life for Danish children, with no empirical material of its own.

Results: Sees the socialisation of the child as a result of the social conditions, which the child and its parents live under.

* * *

Dreier, O. (1977). *Familieværen og bevidsthed. En analyse af en familie i behandling*/Family Being and Consciousness. An Analysis of a Family Under Treatment. Hellerup: Dansk Psykologisk Forlag, 1977. ISBN 87-87580-03-9. In Danish.

Summary: A study of one family under treatment, but with a view to finding connections between internal roles and relations in families and external societal conditions.

Theoretical frame of reference: Critical psychology. Denmark's most advanced.

Method employed: A qualitative analysis of one family corresponding to the theoretical frame of reference. The empirical data are used to illustrate theoretical points and arguments.

Results: The role of the father in the family is regulated by the general and social forms of wage labour. The role of the mother is regulated by the socially determined, privatised forms of housework and the mother function. These external categories regulate the interaction between the adults in the family, their ways of being together and the adults' relations to the children.

* * *

Erdman, B. [et al.] (1985). Småbørns hverdagsliv/The Everyday Life of Young Children. In C. Bøgh & P. Schultz Jørgensen (red.), *Småbørn - familie - samfund. En antologi om småbørnsforskning*/Young children - Family - Society. An Anthology About Research on Young Children. København: Hans Reitzels Forlag. ISBN 87-412-3855-9. In Danish.

Summary: A survey of the social and empirical conditions of child-minding in the family and in the daycare centre.

Theoretical frame of reference: Inspired by critical psychology.

Method employed: Three empirical phases: Journal data regarding children let down by childminding instances. Interviews/observations in kindergartens. Interviews with and diary notes by new mothers. The preparation is qualitative and (so far) "illustrative".

Results: Only data from kindergartens: Traits of childminding show indistinctness on the part of the adults concerning certainty/uncertainty, keeping distance/pawing and break/continuity. The writers conclude that childhood is specifically characterised by considerable ambiguity and uncertainty in the adults' (the pedagogues') daily contact with the children.

* * *

Glavind, N. & J. V. Pedersen (1981). *Arbejdsmiljørapport: Pædagoger i daginstitution*/Working Environment Report: Pedagogues in Daycare Centres. København: Børn & Unge. ISBN 87-87433-37-0. In Danish

Summary: Research of problems concerning the working environment in daycare centres, where illness, physical environment, mental strains, pedagogical possibilities, degree of employment and manning are brought into focus.

Theoretical frame of reference: Not explicitly expressed, but a sociological approach directed by an empirical survey of a new field.

Method employed: 1977-data from a questionnaire survey, statistically prepared.

Results: Stress: 54% often felt stressed, the leader group felt most stressed. Back problems: 47% had one or more back problems. Colds: 22% often caught colds. Attrition: Ill health culminates after 8-10 years, only the robust continue to work in the profession, those who are less robust seek another job after a short span of years. Physical conditions: A combination of many specific factors constitutes a bad working environment. Working hours and children: Pedagogues who work part-time are less stressed than those who work full-time. The authors recommend smaller groups of children, but the political development in Denmark indicates a development in the opposite direction.

* * *

Grønhøj. B. & P. Schultz Jørgensen (1984). *Den familieorienterede daginstitution*/The Family Orientated Daycare Centre. København: Socialforskningsinstituttet. ISBN 87-7487-253-2. In Danish.

Summary: A study of an extended cooperation with parents in two Danish daycare centres.

Theoretical frame of reference: Not explicitly expressed, but a sociological approach directed by importance attached to the empirical side.

Method employed: Existing data about children, parents and pedagogical theoretical frames of reference etc. Telephone interviews with parents. Intensive interviews carried out in 1983 and observations in institutions. The treatment of the data is mainly qualitative, for example, the case method.

Results: The strengthening of parental cooperation demands considerable resources on the part of the parents and the willingness of the pedagogues to give up rights. This can cause difficulties. According to the authors, another model which attaches more importance to the professional role of the pedagogue and operates with extension of the contact surface to the parents, is more agreeable to parental resources. The success of parental cooperation is therefore ultimately dependent on the social conditions arising from the relations between parents and pedagogues.

* * *

Grønhøj, B. (1981). *Småbørns dagpasning: Et problem for forældre og kommuner*/Daycare of Preschool Children: A Parental and Municipal Problem. København: Socialforskningsinstituttet, 103. ISBN 87-7487-190-0. In Danish. With an English summary and abstract.

Summary: A survey aiming to elucidate and compare the family with preschool children with respect to daycare centres, use of other forms of childcare and the parents' satisfaction with respect to the kind of childcare they use.

Theoretical frame of reference: Not explicitly expressed, but a sociological approach directed by importance attached to the empirical side.

Method employed: Questionnaires sent to the parents of 3.754 0-2 and 3-5(6) year-old children. The preparation is statistical and quantitative.

Results: The father's traditional role as the main supporter is unshaken, regardless of the family conditions, as such. The rate of employment of the mothers varies more than in the case of the fathers. However, the younger the child is, the greater the variety in spite of a lower level of public service. In 1975 single mothers had paid work more frequently than mothers in two-parent families. Children in daycare centres come from relatively better socio-economical conditions, than those looked after in the home by the parents. The parents prefer public daycare to private. With regard to mothers with jobs outside the home, there are quite a number of those working full-time, who want part-time work and more time for the family. (Concerning the figures of children in daycare in Denmark in %: The results of the survey are outdated).

* * *

Grünbaum, L. (1977). *Forældre og pædagoger*/Parents and Pedagogues. Hellerup: Dansk Psykologisk Forlag. ISBN 87-87580-05-5. In Danish.

Summary: An analysis of problems and possibilities in the cooperation between parents and pedagogues, theoretically illustrated and with empirical examples from a kindergarten.

Theoretical frame of reference: Organisational psychology. The kindergarten is an organisation, and the correlative parent-pedagogue relations are seen in the light of institutions' social functions (sociology and social-psychology).

Method employed: Unstructured interviews with pedagogues in groups. Thematic qualitative preparation. With data to illustrate theoretical points.

Results: The kindergarten fulfils a number of social functions. Parents and personnel are correlatively dependent because of the child. There exist a number of differences between parents and pedagogues, which manifest themselves in ambivalence and opposition.

* * *

Johansen, E. & L. Thøisen (1983). *Barndom-ungdom. Eksempler på den lange vej gennem institutionerne*/Childhood-Adolescence. Examples of the Long Way Through the Institutions. København: Social- og Sundhedspolitiske Gruppe. ISBN 87-981104-8-9. In Danish.

Summary: An analysis of children's and youths' conditions of rearing in modern society and the deeper connection between capitalistic society's disciplining of the coming labour force and socialisation in the institutions.

Theoretical frame of reference: A capitallogically inspired analysis with a very distinct theoretically based critique of public institutions.

Method employed: A theoretical method with no empirical data of its own: Evaluates others' material.

Results: Childhood is regulated by society's "external disciplining" mediated by the social state, bureaucratisation and the physical splitting up of everyday life. The hidden curriculum of the day-care centres is estimated to be very critical toward the socialisation of children. For instance, the scarcity of contact, of space, of choices, the pedagogues being wage earners the emotional distance that follows from this. This socialises the children independently of the pedagogue's conscious intentions.

* * *

Juul Jensen, J. & O. Langsted (1982). *Integrerede institutioner. Beskrivelse af 14 integrerede institutioner i Århus kommune*/Integrated Institutions. A Description of 14 Integrated Institutions in the Municipality of Århus. Århus: BUPL & PMF, Århus Kommunekreds. ISBN (87-981263-1-8). In Danish.

Summary: A survey describing 14 age-integrated institutions in the municipality of Århus with regard to the physical conditions and the personnel's evaluation of their daily workplace.

Theoretical frame of reference: Not explicitly expressed, but a sociologically orientated, descriptive survey: Segregation among other things based on age, a societally created phenomenon.

Method employed: A questionnaire implemented in 1979, of the number of children, physical conditions, age composition, etc. Interviews with personnel in groups, about their evaluation of advantages/disadvantages of age-integration. The adaption is qualitative, but quantitatively anchored.

Results: Basic thesis: Integrated institutions constitute a counter-tendency against the societal segregation of age groups and the division of children's and adults' everyday life. Personnel: Estimate as positive the opportunity to follow the children for a number of years, that they have a better contact with the parents, that being together with children of different ages, they must show more sides of themselves, that inside the institution they can rotate to new work areas, for instance, being with infants. This brings variety into their work and an all-round knowledge about children. Dissatisfaction concerns low budgets and limited physical conditions. This can change the above mentioned positively estimated signs of the age-integrated institution into negative, because of the often increased strains.

* * *

Jørgensen, M. & P. Schreiner (1985). *Fighterrelationen. Børns kamp mod voksne*/The Fighter Relation. Children's Fight Against Adults. København: Hans Reitzels Forlag.

Summary: An analysis and description of the "new" childhood type: the fighter child, who fights against adults is restless and dashes around. The first Danish book about this subject.

Theoretical frame of reference: Social-relations analysis based on a theoretical approach with the greatest importance attached to external behavioral relations.

Method employed: Theoretical method, no survey, but many consultant experiences.

Results: This type of child is considered to be a result of the "modern way of living". The parents' busyness and tiredness and their feelings of guilt causes weakness and fluctuation in relation to the demands of the child. Especially psychologists, pedagogues and others from the new middle-classes, who have "language as a tool" are supposed to have more fighter children than others.

* * *

Korremann, G. (1977). *Børnehave og socialisering. Om kvinders erhvervsomfang og børnehavens udvikling i Danmark efter 1960*/Kindergarten and Socialisation. About Women's Rate of Employment and the Development of the Kindergarten in Denmark After 1960. København: Gyldendal. ISBN 87-01-54701-1. In Danish.

Summary: A survey of socialization in four Danish kindergartens in the 1970ies.

Theoretical frame of reference: Sociological and social-psychological approach, with a point of departure in theories about stratified socialisation.

Method employed: Expanded theory and a smaller quantitatively and qualitatively prepared survey based on interviews and observations in four kindergartens.

Results: Pedagogue-child communication amounts to three sentences or less in more than 80% of the cases. The observations showed great differences between the children's behaviour in two kindergartens. This is interpreted as a result of different pedagogical practices: Restlessness/conflict is to a high degree connected with "diffuse" pedagogy, while a minimum of restlessness/conflict has a background a practice with many activities in and outside the kindergarten organised by the adults. Aggression is seen as a result of stratified socialisation: Children of working-class parents are bodily more aggressive, which is interpreted as being coherent with the working-classes' "more physical and aggressive child rearing practice".

* * *

Kyng, B. (1974). *Opvækstvilkår og udvikling. En børnepsykologisk forløbsundersøgelse af 65 børn i førskolealderen*/The Rearing Conditions and Development. A Child-psychological Survey of the Progress of 65 Children of Preschool Age. København: Gyldendal. ISBN 00-713112. In Danish.

Summary: A survey of the intellectual development of 0-6 year-old children in relation to the socio-economic status and child rearing practice of the parents.

Theoretical frame of reference: Anchored in clinical child psychology and based on psychoanalysis with the interpersonal relationship (mother-child) brought into focus.

Method employed: Based on structured interviews and series of psychological intelligence- and personality tests. The preparation is statistical and quantitative.

Results: Higher socio-economically placed children score higher on intelligence tests than children from lower strata. There is a relation between the mother's satisfaction with her marriage and the level of intelligence of the child. First-born girls, especially from lower strata, have the greatest number of personality problems in preschool age. Encouragement to independence was related to a higher score of intelligence by the children. In spite of difference in the child rearing practice, 64 out of 65 children were bodily punished by the parents.

* * *

Kyng, B. (1979). *Pilotprojekt vuggestue - dagpleje 1*/Pilot Project Day Nursery - Childminding. Århus: Psykologisk Institut. Psykologisk Skriftserie, 5, 5. In Danish.

Summary: Research (the only one in Denmark) that studies the behaviour of the child and the adult-child relationship with a view to a comparison of day nursery and childminding.

Theoretical frame of reference: Developmental psychology anchored in American interaction theory and empiri and in clinical, psychoanalytical child psychology.

Method employed: Qualitative analysis of open semi-structured observations of 8 children in day nurseries and 8 children in childminding. However, quantitative conclusions of the type, "More or less of this, or that..."

Results: As many essential variations can be found within day nurseries and childminding as between the different day nurseries and childminding. One area, though, showed considerable differences: the children's mutual contact. In the day nurseries the contacts were both fewer and quite brief, whereas, in childminding, they were both more frequent and quite prolonged and substantial. The direction of the interpretation is, that childminding, with its relatively smaller and agewise, more mixed group results in closer contact among the children.

* * *

Nissen, M. (1984). *Skilsmisser og børn. En bog for forældre*/Divorce and Children. A Book for Parents. København: Nyt Nordisk Forlag: ISBN 87-17-05199-1. In Danish.

Summary: Research of how children experience and react to divorce.

Theoretical frame of reference: Not explicitly expressed, but social-psychological approach and a psychological interpretation not characterised by any particular school.

Method employed: An account of the author's own and of others' research. Detailed reference to American research (the author's other publications about divorce have been omitted or have been given a low priority in this biography, as they are about children older than six years).

Results: Each year 18,000-19,000, Danish children are exposed to divorce. Not many of them understand the background for the divorce. Research of 0-6 year-olds show that they react with irritability, anger, tears and confusion. Many have sleep problems and are afraid to be alone. Between 5-6 years there are feelings of guilt and self-reproach. The children have difficulties in working out their feelings. 5-6 year-olds begin to understand and can to a higher degree express loss and sadness and wish for reunion of the parents.

* * *

Schousbøl, I. (1985). Man kommer ikke sovende til børn, der udvikler selvbestemmelse/One Does Not Get Children, Who Develop Self-determination Without Any Effort of One's Own. In C. Bøgh & P. Schultz Jørgensen (red.), *Småbørn - family -samfund*/Young Children - Family - Society. København: Hans Reitzels Forlag. ISBN 87-412-3855-9. In Danish.

Summary: A survey of young children's self-determination and adults' related socialisation strategies.

Theoretical frame of reference: Critical psychology attempting to connect societal conditions with child rearing practice in families and daycare centres.

Method employed: Qualitative interviews and observations of a number of 4-5 year-olds at home and in the kindergarten. The preparation is qualitatively descriptive.

Results: Some children thrive in Denmark in the 1980ies. The child rearing aim of the parents is to give the child zest for life and to bring them up to "be themselves" emotionally. The most important impulses come from the parents' own life, both past and present, where they recognise themselves in the child. The families in the survey (the middle-classes) are characterised as "developmentally oriented".

* * *

Sigsgaard, E. (1984). *Børn og voksne - et fælles liv. Bd. 1-4*/Children and Adults - a Common Life, Vol. 1-4. København: Tiderne skifter. ISBN 87-7445-175-8. In Danish.

Summary: 4 books about the extension of cooperation between children, parents and pedagogues in four daycare centres. Describes and evaluates the different sides the splitting up of of everyday life and gives guidelines for a so-called "countercurrent".

Theoretical frame of reference: The point of origin is a socialistic socio-critical analysis and the pedagogy must - even if it is not explicitly expressed - be a so-called disengaging pedagogy, where the accent is placed on overcoming the separation and a non-interventional attitude to the adult-child relation.

Results: Many, but in abstracts: Pedagogy and socialisation must have its point of origin in children's rebellion and protest against separation. Family and daycare centre must support and supplement each other regarding the child. Fantasy and the child's need of activity is a liberating power, which adults must open up for and not lock in. If this is successful, these children will, as future adults, contribute to remove socially created compulsion and destruction of human fellowship.

* * *

Småbørn, *daginstitutioner og dagpleje* (1980)/Young Children, Daycare Centres and Childminding. København: Børnekommissionen. Udvalgsrapport, 2. ISBN 87-503-3201-5. In Danish.

Summary: An analysis of and suggestions for improvement of infant care in daycare centres and childminding. Evaluates the aim and development of the centre and looks at laws and regulations, at the physical frames and at the structure of the municipal daycare. Matters of internal personnel and parental cooperation with regard to the organisation of the pedagogical work is examined. Furthermore, the economic conditions regarding the daycare centres' use of public money is discussed.

Theoretical frame of reference: Not explicitly expressed, but within an interdisciplinary sociological frame.

Method employed: An analysis of existing material and research. With no empirical material of its own.

Results: In spite of an increase during the 1970ies in the number of daycare centres, the demand indicates that even if the child-minding is taken care of in another way, more parents prefer to have their children in a daycare centre, than can be accommodated. The development of daycare centres has shifted from private to public enterprise. The development has also progressed from meeting the social demand to include offers of a more pedagogical kind. According to the law, the local council is bound to provide the "necessary" number of places in daycare centres for children and youngsters. The committee finds that this does not imply that there has to be place for "all" children and youngsters. In the interplay between the pedagogue and the child, the size of the group and its composition are decisive. The ideal amount of time for the child to stay in a centre is not more than 6 hours a day. Great importance is ascribed to the interplay between the institution and the local environment. Extension of age-integrated centres is recommended, but without economising on personnel. The physical environment is of decisive importance for the pedagogue and the planning of the outdoor areas must to a higher degree be adapted to the development of young children. The advantages and disadvantages of childminding are expounded. The committee suggests that: Daycare be limited to children under 3 years of age who have a special need for contact. Obligatory education/training of childminders and guidelines with a view to obtaining a greater degree of homogeneity are recommended. Parents must be ensured influence, as they are in daycare centres. Regarding the daily work in the centres, the committee recommends, that this should not be bound by legislation but rather, that general pedagogical guidelines should be published by the civil authority.

* * *

Sommer, D. (1984). *Når far er hjemme. Om faderrollen, fædre og spædbørn*/When Daddy is at Home. About the Father Role, Fathers and Infants. Hellerup: Dansk Psykologisk Forlag. ISBN: 87-87580-75-6. In Danish.

Summary: An analysis of the father role in society, in the family and in the individual man's mentality, with a view to acquiring an understanding of the specific empirically ascertainable father-infant relations.

Theoretical frame of reference: Eclectical level-model with the material frames as a point of origin of the understanding of role changes and psychological conditions.

Method employed: Theoretical method with a discussion of the theory and research of others.

Results: The father role has been changing in recent decades, but there is still inequality between women and men regarding the division of housework and the responsibility of childcare. Research indicates that in spite of this, the fathers show considerable qualities in their interaction with the infants. The mother myth has blocked recognition of this. If real changes in the prevailing traditional roles are to take place, there must be changes in society and not least, changes in both men's and women's deep personal attitudes.

* * *

Sommer, D. (1985). Familiedannelse. Psykiske problemer hos forældre med et nyfødt barn. Establishing a Family. Psychological Problems of Parents With a New-born Child. In C. Bøgh & P. Schultz Jørgensen (red.), *Småbørn - familie - samfund. En antologi om småbørnsforskning*/Young Children - Family - Society. An Anthology About Research on Young Children. København: Hans Reitzels Forlag. ISBN: 87-412-3855-9. In Danish.

Summary: A survey of the fathers' and mothers' psychological difficulties in connection with family establishment.

Theoretical frame of reference: The family is seen as an unity of interaction and communication in relation to external material reality (system-theoretically inspired approach).

Method employed: A quantitative description and a qualitative interpretation of semi-structured interviews with 20 families. Collection of data 1980-81.

Results: A large majority of mothers and every second father report extensive psychological depressions and/or fluctuations in one or several periods from the birth of the child until 5 months later. This is supported by surveys using "impressionistic" statements of respondents. Qualitative analysis interprets this as the child's imperative intervention in the life of the couple, changes in the couple's relationship, the isolation of the family from the network and the intensification of the internal and external work strain.

* * *

Transgaard, H. (1982). *Nye holdninger til børnepasning. Holdningsændringer blandt småbørnsmødre 1975-1979*/New Attitudes Towards Childcare. Changes of Attitude Among Mothers of Young Children 1975-1979. København: Socialforskningsinstituttet. Studie, 43. ISBN 87-7487-214-1. In Danish.

Summary: A survey of attitudes towards forms of childcare with a view to explaining a demand for daycare centres in the 1970's unexpected by society.

Theoretical frame of reference: Not explicitly expressed, but a sociological approach with importance attached to the empirical side.

Method employed: Structured interviews with 470 mothers with young children in 1975 and with 245 mothers in 1979. The preparation is both quantitative and statistical.

Results: The proportion of mothers who look upon part-time kindergarten as the best form of childcare has grown from 1/2 in 1975 to 2/3 in 1979. The proportion who preferred childcare at home all day, has fallen from 1/3 to 1/4 during the same period. This can be interpreted - relatively independent of the necessity of paid work - as if mothers in 1979 look upon public childcare as the most attractive caring form.

* * *

Weltzer, H. (1985). Teaching Infants Infant-Infant Interaction. *Early Child Development and Care, 20, 145-155.* In English.

Summary: A Survey highlighting a developmental description and carried out with the purpose of building up a conscious pedagogical practice concerning 0-3 year-old children. Conducted in a day nursery in Aarhus.

Theoretical frame of reference: Developmental-psychological An eclectical model developed by dr. Kuno Beller.

Method employed: Quantitative, structured observations of the infant, and of infant-infant interaction. Also qualitative descriptions of the practice based, for example, on video recordings.

Results: The social behavior of infants exists far earlier than should theoretically be expected. Pedagogically conscious aims for the development of the children are a decisive link in the socialisation of infants.

* * *

Ørum, T. (red.) (1977). *Mens de voksne arbejder - om børn og daginstitutioner*/While Adults Work - About Children and Day-Care Centres. Dragør: Tiderne Skifter. In Danish.

Summary: Different authors elucidate how modern childhood has evolved and its present state. Daycare centres in capitalist society are analysed with respect to content, aims and pedagogy. Aspects of the education of pedagogues, their qualifications and a (negative) view of daycare are presented.

Theoretical frame of reference: Various, since there are contributions by different authors, but a common critical attitude towards capitalism. Psychologically, the contributions cover the spectrum from psychoanalysis to Soviet psychology. This is typical of the Danish scene, where two "left-wing pedagogies" are struggling to become the leading ideology on the pedagogical market in the 1970's and the 1980's.

Method employed: Theoretical with no empirical data of its own. This is also characteristic of the Danish pedagogical atmosphere where the professional discussion is mainly based on theory, and, where young children's and others reality is interpreted deductively. For example, the formulation of the conception of practice is particularly theoretical.

Results: Many - a few here: Modern childhood evolved with the historical removal of the child from societal production and thereby from his/her common life-context with adults. The life of the child became a life of the intimate sphere, and the daycare centres were created as an answer to the isolation of the children from society, etc.

* * *

YOUNG CHILDREN'S CULTURAL CONDITIONS

Brostrøm, S. & K. Rasmussen (1981). *En nødvendig pædagogik - dialektisk, struktureret pædagogik. Introduktion og videre-udvikling/*A Necessary Pedagogy - Dialectical, Structured Pedagogy. Introduction and Further Development. København: Børn og Unge: ISBN: 87-87433-36-2. In Danish.

Summary: The basis of pedagogy in children's life conditions under capitalism. Point of origin in Soviet psychology and Makarenko-pedagogy as the basis for the preparation of the "necessary" structured pedagogy in the kindergarten.

Theoretical frame of reference: An attempt is made to transfer Soviet psychology and -pedagogy to another, capitalistic society.

Method employed: Theoretical method with no empirical data of its own. The most common method used in the pedagogical struggle among "schools" in Denmark.

Results: An intimate connection between children's societal conditions under capitalism and their needs, ways of perception and acting. Pedagogy must have its point of origin in the adults' knowledge of this and to a lesser extent, in the child's own everyday experiences. The child does not develop according to inner laws. Therefore, child rearing must create an external structure for the child's everyday life. Relatively adult intervening pedagogy.

* * *

Felding, J., N. Møller & S. Schmidt (1980). *Pædagogik og barndom/*Pedagogy and Childhood. København: Unge Pædagoger. Serie, B 24. ISBN: 87-87400-36-7. In Danish.

Summary: An important contribution to the Danish debate on pedagogy in the light of the child's conditions in society.

Theoretical frame of reference: Critical theory, experience pedagogy - a socialist alternative to the structured, Soviet orientated pedagogy.

Method employed: Theoretical method, not an empirical study.

Results: Childhood and capitalism are inseparable. Children are looked upon as potential rebels. Everyday life is split up, which has a negative effect on the socialisation of the child, pedagogy and socialisation must be based on the child's experience of its own everyday life in order to have a liberating effect. Pedagogy is a dialectical process between the pedagogue and the child and must be conducted as a relatively non-intervening practice on part of the adult.

* * *

Fischer, U., L. Madsen & B. Leicht (1984). *Se her! En bog om børns opmærksomhed*/Look here! A Book About Preschool Children's Attention. København: Børn og Unge. ISBN: 87-87433-52-4. In Danish.

Summary: Developmental work in the kindergarten highlighting the consequences for the children of the adults' control in proportion to the children's capacity for attention.

Theoretical frame of reference: Not quite clear but it is pointed out that contributions are made both to the "constructivist" school (Piaget) and to the "cultural-historical" school (here, especially Vygotsky).

Method employed: Participant observation and video recordings. The preparation is carried out together with the pedagogues (developmental work) according to a thematic, qualitative method.

Results: The feeling of "chaos" experienced by the pedagogues is often not consistent with a more objective interpretation. Control by the pedagogues, for example, via use of structured topic centered work, disciplines the children according to the logic of adults and is therefore often quite out of step with the rules regulating the attention of the preschool child.

* * *

Poulsgaard, K. (1979). *Socialisering og frigørende pæda-gogik*/Socialisation and Disengaging Pedagogy. København: Ejlers forlag. ISBN: 87-7241-444-8. In Danish.

Summary: An analysis of socialisation research (the conventional) seen in a historical-societal perspective with a view to assessment disengaging pedagogy.

Theoretical frame of reference: The cultural-historical school as a psychological basis of understanding the child's activities in a general perspective.

Method employed: Theoretical method with no empirical data of its own.

Results: Traditional socialisation research has too narrow a view of child rearing and pedagogy, as it wants to adjust the child to the established order. The aim of disengaging pedagogy is to emancipate the child from the compulsions of society, and it must be founded on a scientifically consistent, holistic dialectical-materialistic view on the child.

* * *

FINNISH BIBLIOGRAPHY

YOUNG CHILDREN'S MATERIAL CONDITIONS

Alanen, L. (1980). *Aikuisten toiminta ja toimintojen yhteydet lapsiperheissä*/The Activities of Adults and Their Connections With the Activities Within Families With Children. Tampere: University of Tampere. The Institute of Social Science, serie A: 52. ISBN 951-44-0976-0. ISSN 0358-0237. In Finnish.

Summary: The intention in the empirical part of the survey is to show 1) The connections between the general conditions determined by the parents' paid work, by the kind of work by other factors connected with the work and the activities of the parents in other fields. 2) How their roles as intermediaries and the independence in the structure of the children's activities vary with the objective traits of the work of the parents, of the connection of the activities of the parents besides their paid work and of how the subjective experience of the importance of the work corresponds with the parents' roles as intermediaries and with the independence in the structure of the children's own activities.

Theoretical frame of reference: A marxist approach.

Method employed: Two samples; one with 212 families with one 6 year-old child from four different geographical locations. Questionnaires, interviews and time-use formulas.

Results: In families with children, the activities of the parents determined by the work are very unequal for the mothers and fathers. Compared with the fathers, the mothers have a structure of activities, that is determined less by the general conditions of the work and by the kind of work. In the families with 6 year-olds the general traits of the work (the place of work, the working hours, the form of salary) and the kind of job (its social character, how binding it is and so on) are reflected to a higher degree in other activites by the fathers than by the mothers. Even if they have a paid job, mothers in families with children are so tied to their functions as housewives as long as the children are small, that, to them, the work sector is a seperate sector. The parents' general working conditions and especially the social character of the father's job, has a statistical connection with the degree to which the family life is isolated from these activities and with how varied family life is.

* * *

Carlson, J. (1975). *Salokylän kuusivuotias*/To Be 6 Years Old In a Sparsely Built Up Area. Helsinki: University of Helsinki. Master thesis in sociology. In Finnish.

Summary: A social-anthropological description of the behavioural habits of 6 year-olds in North Karelian. The research is, among other things, meant to be the basis of preschool planning in sparsely built up areas. The position of institutions relevant for 6 year-olds has also been looked into.

Theoretical frame of reference: The social-behavioural view of the child as the product of its social way of acting and its relevant environment. The author attempts to overcome the perceptions of the child as "completely formed by the environment" and "as an active and creative individual". With a point of departure in the social-behavioural point of view, the social life of the 6 year-olds is described as an element of the social constitution that makes the child a member of its culture.

Method employed: Active observation.

Results: Importance is attached to factors describing the environment in a sparsely built up area. The long distances and nature are pointed out as both delimiting and possibility-creating factors and as important for the behavioural patterns of the 6 year-olds. Illness also characterises everyday life. Loneliness is a factor usually paid too little attention.

* * *

Halla, K. (1982). *Yksinhuoltajien asema ja ongelmat*/The Position and Problems of Single Breadwinners in Finland. In Official Statistics of Finland. Special Social Studies, XXXII:82. Helsinki: Ministry of Social Affairs and Health. Research Department. ISBN 951-46-6163-x. In Finnish. With a summary in English.

Summary: A survey of the living conditions and problems of single breadwinners and especially of the difficulties encountered by those in the worst positions.

Theoretical frame of reference: A practical, social political approach.

Method employed: Questionnaires from 1977 of 1492 single breadwinners living with at least one child under the age of 18 and of 250 couples of whom, one parent was living with the child and the other was responsible for the support of the child.

Results: 10% of the single breadwinners lived in accommodations without any basic conveniences. Single breadwinners with a low income were primarily part of the economically inactive population and received supplementary benefits more often than families with both parents living together. 23% of the single-parent families had children under school age. Only 7% in this group were satisfied with their childcare arrangements. The majority of children in single-parent families were looked after in municipal daycare centres. The children of single breadwinners, who worked irregular hours lacked suitable childcare provisions. If the child was born out of wedlock, the fathers very rarely visited their children and more than half of them had never visited the child. The corresponding figure for divorced fathers was 30%. The position of single breadwinners worsened with low material standard of living and low social status. Half of the single breadwinners had practically no leisure time and one in ten experienced other people's attitudes towards them as unfavourable. The economic position of the single-parent family was better than that of the parent responsible for paying for the support of the child.

* * *

Nummenmaa, A.-R. (1981). *Isä alle kouluikäisen lapsen yksinhuoltajana*/The Father as a Single Breadwinner With a Child Under School Age. Tampere: University of Tampere. Reports from the Department of Psychology. ISBN 951-44-1184-6. In Finnish.

Summary: Part of a survey the aim of which is to elucidate the early interaction between the child and the father and its development. The emphasis in this part of the survey, is especially placed on the interpretation of the child's behaviour as a condition of understanding interaction.

Theoretical frame of reference: With a basis in different socialisation theories: The psychoanalytic developmental theory, Parson's theory and theories of learning (Bandura, Bandura & Walters).

Method employed: A sample of 13 male single breadwinners, who had custody of at least one child under school age and who lived in Tampere during the survey. "Thematic interviews" with 32 main questions. Descriptive analysis.

Results: The maternal contact was sparse, only 3 out of 10 had regular visitating arrangements. With the exception of one child, they were looked after outside the home (10 in daycare centres and 2 in private childminding). The activities together with the father were concentrated around the week-ends. On the basis of the interaction in the families, these were divided into 3 groups: 1) Families with very good interaction based on an understanding of the development and the needs of the child (3). 2) Families with less interaction than the first group. The fathers, though, are together with their children and show interest in them (4). 3) Families with few common activities. In the first group the fathers had applied for custody, they had conscious rearing principles and viewed being together with the child as positive. In group 3, half of the fathers became single breadwinners more or less against their will, as the mother had left the family. Their rearing principles were more confused than in the first group. The experiences of the fathers were not differentiated.

* * *

Nummenmaa, A.-R. (1978). *Perheen työaikarakenne ja lapsen kehity-sehdot*/The Structure of the Family's Working Hours and the Child's Developmental Conditions. Tampere: University of Tampere. Reports from the Department of Psychology. ISBN 951-9311-80-7. ISSN 0359-1808. In Finnish.

Summary: Three aspects were examined: 1) Conditions of importance for the children's evening and night care. How great is the demand and, who needs it? 2) How does the parents' working irregular hours influence the development of the child? 3) What can the different models of evening and night care offer the families and, how do these rearing environments influence the child?

Theoretical frame of reference: A practical approach.

Method employed: Interviews with and questionnaires of the parents, the daycare personnel and the childminders. The sample consisted of 543 families with children under school age. Assessments and observations of the children and the daycare centres. A follow-up study one year after, of the development of the child and of the childcare arrangements. The test group consisted of 151 families, where at least one of the parents worked irregular hours. A control group of families, in which the parents worked during the day.

Results: Problems concerning minding the children caused by irregular working hours, implies an unsteady rearing environment: different places, a variety of daily childcare arrangements, an irregular dayrythm and reduced possibilities for the family to participate in activities together. The family daycare is to a large degree the kind of service used by single breadwinners, with day-, evening- and night shift. The families are also forced to use other forms of childcare. In families with irregular working hours, the predominant form of childcare was being taken care of in the home. Of those working day shift, 8% were dependent on two or more arrangements, if working evening-shift, the figure was 25% and working night shift, it was 8%. Unfavourable conditions of development were accumulated in single breadwinner families or families in which the parents worked two different shifts. A centre functioning day and night stabilised the childcare situation for nearly all the families. For the children it meant development and new friends, but in the beginning, also adjustment difficulties, bad habits and retarded development.

* * *

Rajala, K. & I. Ruoppila (1983). *Nuori lapsiperhe*/The Young Family With Children. Helsinki: Mannerheimin Lastensuojeluliiton lapsiraportti, A42. ISBN 951-9311-89-0. ISSN O359-1808. In Finnish, and belonging to the same project:

Stranden, P. & I. Ruoppila (1982). *Nuori lapsiperhe: tutkimus nuorten perheiden elämäntilanteesta ja toimintaedellytyksistä*/The Young Family With Children: A Study of the Living Conditions and Assumption of Activities. Helsinki: Mannerheimin Lastensuojeluliiton lapsiraportti, A32. ISBN 951-9311-80-7. ISSN 0359-1808. In Finnish.

Summary: The project "Young Families With Children" has the following aims: To survey the life situation of young families with children (material, social and cultural conditions), to find resources which will enable the parents to manage the tasks of the family and especially the relations in the families and the rearing of the children.

Theoretical frame of reference: A practical social-political approach.

Method employed: A follow-up study. A sample of mothers from nine different geographical locations, all under the age of 24 and all expecting their first child. The sample consists of 63 families (including married, cohabiting and single breadwinners). Questionnaires and interviews.

Results: The life situation: The young parents can be described as family and work orientated. Every third and nearly every second wife had no vocational education. In general, the life situation was unstable. 52% of the young families with children felt that their situation became worse after the birth of the child. 58% of the children of the age of 10-11 months were minded by their parents. The relations within the family: The most important resource, when adapting to the change in the family's life, was a good relationship between the parents. Every fourth mother had ambivalent feelings towards the child. The fathers seemed to be well adapted to the changes. In the families with good relations, the fathers participated more in the caregiving. Every third father had ambivalent feelings towards the child. Generally, the children had good contact with their parents. Rearing: One third of the parents wanted to rear their children in the same way as they themselves had been reared. When the children were 10-11 months old, 60% of the mothers, who had been physically punished themselves, had used milder physical punishment towards their children. Family planning: In the last phase of the study 3 out of 4 parents wanted another child.

* * *

Ritanies, M., O. Riihinen, H. Penttinen & A. Pulkkinen (1984). *Lapsilukuihanne - toive vai tavoite*/The Ideal Number of Children - a Wish or a Goal. Vammala: The Population Research Institute, Helsinki. D 13/1984. ISBN 951-9048-61-8. ISSN 0357-4725. In Finnish.

Summary: A survey of the connection between welfare and the number of children planned and between welfare and the development in the number of children planned.

Theoretical frame of reference: Demographical survey based on the surveys of Phillipe Aries and Ron Lesthaeges.

Method employed: Interviews with a representative sample of 5449 married women aged 19-45.

Results: More than half of the women interviewed considered 2 children ideal in a family, about 1/3 thought that Finnish families ought to have at least 4 children. The general ideal has not decreased in Finland during the 1970ies. The ideal number was

highest among women with an academic education; 2.8 children;
Among women with a middle-range education the number was
the lowest; 2.6 children. The ideal number was lowest among the
middle income classes. Among those for whom religion was very
important, the number was 2.9 and among those who had a negative attitude towards religion, the number was 2.5. The variable
of religion correlated with the variable of region. In the entailed
estate of Uleåborg, the number among religious women was 3.4.
Hindrances for the realization of the ideal number were the
woman's paid job, disagreement among the spouses about the
number and a higher average among the population. Those, who
did not reach the planned number, were families who reduced
the number wanted over the years. 16% of those who did not
have the planned number, had more children than planned. The
final number was highest in the lowest income classes, among
women with a primary school education and in families where
religion was of importance.

* * *

Säntti, R. & H. Väliaho, (1984). *Lapsiperheiden palkaton kotityö:
ajankäyttö ja arvo*/Unpaid Housework in Families With Children:
Time-Use and Value. In Kotityötutkimus, osa IX/Housework study,
part IX. SVT, Official Statistics of Finland. Special Social Studies,
XXXII:84. ISBN 951-46-6212-1. ISSN 0071-5336. In Finnish. With an
English Summary.

Summary: A research project carried out by the Ministry of Social
Affairs and Health, to determine the value of unpaid housework.

Theoretical frame of reference: A social-political approach.

Method employed: Questionnaire.

Results: The average time spent on housework in families with children was 9.2 hours per day. 97.5% of the wives and nearly 75% of
the husbands did some kind of unpaid housework during the period studied. In families, where the parents had an elementary
school background, the amount of work done by children and

other family members was greater than in other families. The time spent by the wives on housework rose to 8.6 hours per day, in families with 2 children of preschool age and to nearly 10 hours per day, if there were 3 or more children under 7 years. The time that the husbands spent on housework, also increased, if the family included preschool children. The husbands of women with jobs away from home, helped their wives on an average of 2.2 hours per day, while the husbands of women with no employment contributed with 2.1 hours. Women living in rural districts spent, on average, one hour more on housework, than women living in cities. Husbands with higher administrative or clerical jobs spent the most time on housework.

* * *

Säntti, R. & U. Husa (1981). *Tiedustelu pienten lasten äideille vuonna 1981*/Enquiries of Mothers of Infants in 1981. Helsingfors: Sosiaali-ja terveysministeriö, 9. ISBN 951-46-5703-9. In Finnish.

Summary: A statement of the conditions of new mothers before and after the birth of the child, their economic situation and their possibilities for choosing between paid work or staying at home and of childcare arrangements.

Theoretical frame of reference: A practical approach.

Method employed: Questionnaire.

Results: 68% of the mothers had paid work before their maternity leave. After the maternity leave 32% of the mothers stayed at home. Whether the mother went back to work or not, was first and foremost a question of economy, for example, because of interest on housing loans and student loans. The second most important reason was, that the mother wanted to keep her place of work. Job satisfaction was mentioned as the third reason. The mothers who stayed at home, mentioned that their most important reason was that they wanted to take care of the child themselves. Two other reasons were difficulties in getting a job and with arrangements for childcare. Of the mothers with paid work, 76% would stay at home, if they had the economic possibilities.

*   *   *

Takala, M. (1986). Family Activity Patterns as Related to the Symmetry in the Division of Labour in the Family, Children's Socialisation to Work and the Significance of Work for the Parents. In *Journal of Psychology of Education, 1, 1. Special print.* In English.

Summary: In the present survey, comparisons were made between families that are homogenous with regard to educational and social status, but differ in the following aspects: Regarding the division of housework and domestic duties between the spouses, the socialisation of the children to work and the parents' role in the cooperation in the family and regarding the relative significance of work versus family life for the family.

Theoretical frame of reference: Within the tradition of life research.

Method employed: A sample of two-parent families with one 6 year-old child. The parents and the children were interviewed separately, each of them twice. The types of families according to the aspects mentioned above, were compared on basis of the activity patterns of the family members and their mutual interaction. In addition to this, the subgroups were compared with regard to the working and living conditions of the parents.

Results: Increased symmetry is related to the wife's employment and to the status and nature of her job. High symmetry and equality between the activities of the spouses is reflected in the number of common activities and interests with the children. The wife's job and working conditions call forth increased participation from the husband. On the other hand, high quality of participation in housework was less related to external conditions and seems more to reflect the relationships within the family. Equality and symmetry were associated with such aspects of family patterns as characterise positive and harmonious interaction.

* * *

YOUNG CHILDREN'S SOCIAL CONDITIONS

Heikkinen, A., T. Markkanen & M. Tanta (1976). *Agression ennaltaekäisy. 1. Lasten itsekontrollin kehittäminen*/Prevention of Aggression. 1. The Development of Children's Self-control. Jyväskylä: University of Jyväskylä. Master thesis in psychology.

Summary: The aim is to develop directions for the prevention of aggressive behaviour.

Theoretical frame of reference: A combination of theories of social learning and phenomenology. Aggression is seen from Lea Pulkkinen's (Pitkänen, 1969) two-dimensional model's point of view. A method of instruction consisting of 32 lessons treating three main subjects: self-understanding, the understanding of others and of the importance of constructive acts.

Method employed: Experiments in two daycare centres with a group of 13 girls and 16 boys aged 4-6 years and with a control group, for a duration of 22 days. Interviews with and observations of the children.

Results: The method of instruction improved the children's self-control without reducing their activity. The method influenced the children's ability to judge situations of different behaviour most successfully. The children had learned to understand themselves and others. The method also influenced the behaviour of the child, most clearly with respect to obeying rules, showing feelings and treating anger and quarreling constructively. The self-control of children, who had originally been judged as aggressive, had improved most.

* * *

Helenius, A. (1982). *Roolileikki ja lasten sosiaaliset suhteet Roolileikin tarkastelu lasten moraalisen kehityksen ja kasvatuksen* *kannalta*/The Role Play and Social Relations of the Child. Jyväskylän yliopisto.

Summary: The content of 5-6 year-olds' spontaneous role play has been analysed. Special attention is drawn to the connection between content of the play, moral development and rearing conditions.

Theoretical frame of reference: Within the cultural-historical school.

Method employed: Material from daycare centres in the German Federal Republic and in Finland. 173 journals of active observations recording the content of play. Analysis of the regulating elements, the themes and and the specific models of the relations of themes and the interaction of the children were made. Estimation criteria have been deduced from the aims of rearing, where the cooperation relations, values and norms appearing in play, creativity and planning ability were variables.

Results: The results showed, that already in play on an average level, many faceted activity relations, in which the child practices the plain and complicated base accomplishments of interaction, can be discovered. The quality of the relations in play can be in harmony or in discord with the aims of rearing. This means that children's spontaneous play can be used in the estimation of how set aims of rearing can be attained. The different themes of role play make different models of relations topical and cause divisions in the quality of the real interaction. The most popular games between boys and girls are strongly attached to the prevailing sex roles. The comparison of the daycare centres in Finland and the Federal Republic of Germany showed that play activities and through this, the conditions of the development of personality and morals, take different forms in an environment with goal-directed rearing.

* * *

Hurme, H. (1981). *Lasten elämänmuutokset*/Life Changes During Childhood. Jyväskylä: Jyväskylän yliopisto. Jyväskylä Studies in Education, Psychology and Social Research, 41. ISSN 0075-4625. ISBN 951-678-462-3. In Finnish. With an English abstract.

Summary: Concerning the instability of the child's environment. Consisting of 4 parts, which cover the most central phases of life-event research. A: Ratings made by 70 Finnish child guidance workers on the readjustment required at 4 age levels by 30 life events. B: Concerns the occurrence of both single life events and indexes of abundant change. C: Concerns their impact. D: Analyses the maternal factors influencing this relationship.

Theoretical frame of reference: Represents the life-event research tradition. Combines features of stress theory, McReynold's theory on the impact of cognitive incongruence and Pulkkinen's theory concerning self-control in children.

Method employed: Ratings by 70 child guidance workers and data were gathered by using thematic interviews. A semi-structured method, partly developed by the author for this study.

Results: A: The death of the mother was rated as the most serious event at all age levels. There were considerable differences among the ratings for the different age-groups. The re-test reliability was very high, about .85. There was a remarkably high correspondence with data obtained in other countries, especially when the wording of the events was identical. B, C, D: Children who had experienced many changes showed low self-control and many behavioural problems. If the mother lacked initiative and respect for social norms, the child often showed low self-control, especially in the high-change group.

* * *

Huttunen, E. & L. Turja (1982). *Avoin päiväkoti osana varhaiskasvatusta. Toimintakokeilun kehittely ja tuloksellisuus*/An Open Daycare Centre as Part of Early Rearing. The Development and Advantage of an Organisational Experiment. Joensuu: Joensuun korkeakoulu, kasvatustieteiden osaston selosteita ja tiedotteita, 33/1982. ISBN 951-696-377-3. In Finnish.

Summary: A study of the basis of the rearing practice in an open daycare centre. A description of an experiment with a model for an open daycare centre in the city of Nurmes. An evaluation of the results of the experiment.

Theoretical frame of reference: The idea of the central role of the family in rearing children according to, among others, Bronfenbrenner's ecological psychology.

Method employed: Action research. A presentation of the results of a longitudinal study of 54 children. Besides questionnaires, also interviews with 20 adult visitors and with the personnel.

Results: The emotional atmosphere in the daycare centre was positive from the beginning. The cooperation and the social contacts between the parents developed. Through counseling and by supporting the parents, their rearing attitudes and -methods were influenced positively. Their rearing skills were fortified and their estimation of their own rearing methods and of their children were more objective than earlier. According to the parents, the behaviour of the children had developed in a positive way during the stay in the daycare centre and according to the personnel, their ability to function in a group and their acquistion of rules had improved. An open daycare centre gathers the families for common activities, carries out preventative work for psychological health and supports the existing daycare activities and rearing in the homes.

* * *

Hämäläinen, H. (1976). *Päiväkoti kasvuympäristönä. Kuvaus päiväkotien toiminnan edellytyksis ja sisällöstä*/The Daycare Centre as a Rearing Environment. A Description of the Conditions and the Content of the Activities of Daycare Centres. Jyväskylä: University of Jyväskylä. Reports from the department of Psychology, 179/1976. ISBN 951-677-635-3. In Finnish.

Socialization of Young Children in the Nordic Countries

Summary: A presentation of the present activities of daycare centres. A general picture of the in- and outside environment, of the play-ground equipment, of the education and number of the personnel and of the size of the groups of children. An evaluation of this according to rearing activities.

Theoretical frame of reference: A practical approach.

Method employed: A questionnaire completed by the personnel and the parents. A diary kept of 2 weeks of the activities in 42 daycare centres, of which 34 were situated in cities and 8 in villages.

Results: Both the personnel and the parents set up aims of rearing and activities in the daycare centre. The activities of the daycare centres are rather multifarious and are to a certain degree, deficient in consequence and outline. The following is recommended: The principles of activity-plans must be defined and the methods of rearing in groups clarified. The daily functions in the daycare centres and those occurring now and then, must be differentiated and their importance must be evaluated in regard to the existing knowledge of the development of the child, to the aims of rearing and to the creation of an adequate day- and week arrangement.

* * *

Ikonen-Nylund, M. (1979). *Perhepävanhoitaja ja hoitolapset. Perhepäivähojien ammattipersoonallisuutta ja hoitalasten suhdetta hoitajiinsa käsittelevä tutkimus*/Childminding and the Child in Childminding. A Survey of the Job Satisfaction of Childminders and of the Children's Relations to Their Minders. Helsinki: University of Helsinki. Master thesis in psychology. In Finnish.

Summary: A survey of whether the job satisfaction, the self-perception and the rearing attitudes of the childminders and the mothers differ and whether it is possible to explain the difference by means of a model of the traditional versus the radical woman's-role. Besides this, attention was drawn to factors influencing the child's affections for their minders.

Theoretical frame of reference: With a point of departure in Rita Liljeström's model of the traditional versus the radical woman's-role.

Method employed: Questionnaire of and interviews with the mothers and childminders of 36 children, who had reached the age of 3. Furthermore the children were tested by a special version of the Family Relations Test, worked out for this survey.

Results: The childminders were placed closer to the extreme traditional on the continuum traditional-radical woman's-role, than the mothers were. The FRT showed that generally, the affection of the children was concentrated on the mother. Only 3.1% of both positive and negative feelings were attributed to the childminder. The results indicate that if a child is in the situation where the atmosphere in the home is off balance, then it needs to attach its affection to a substitute for the mother.

* * *

Jallonija, R. (1976). *Tutkimus lasten päivähoidon kehityspiirteistä Suomessa*/A Survey of the Development of Daycare in Finland. Helsinki: University of Helsinki. Department of Sociology. Papers I, 1976. ISBN 951-45-0998-6. In Finnish.

Summary: A survey of the existence of different kinds of daycare for children under school age in Finland and of the connection of the daycare forms and society and the material conditions of production. The position of the family and of the woman is seen as a result of the development of production.

Theoretical frame of reference: The materialistic concept of history and the theory of capitalism is used in a general description of the tendencies of the subject studied. The daycare forms (daycare centre and childminding) are observed in the light of the crucial conception of this survey.

Method employed: Correlations and part-correlations have been included on the one hand, among a number of variables characterising the power of a societal development in the municipals and on the other hand, the development of the daycare in a societal direction.

Results: During the earliest time of capitalism and also later on, it was mostly the mothers who took care of the children, this means that this aspect of the division of labour has been very stable during the reign of capitalism. This state of affairs continued until 1950, when the daycare was effected by the population increase in the beginning of the 1950ies. But still 50% of the families in the cities and 59% in the municipals minded their children as part of the housework. If relatives are included, the figures become 63%, and 73% respectively. This "undevelopment" of daycare is partly due to the fact, that there have always been alternatives, such as relatives and bigger sisters and brothers.

* * *

Keskinen, S. (1985). *Päiväkotihenkilöstön työtyytyväisyys ja psyykkinen hyvinvointi/*Job Satisfaction and Psychological Well-being of Daycare Personnel. Turku: Turun yliopisto. Psykologian tutkimuksia 76/1985. ISBN 951-642-719-7. In Finnish. With an English Summary.

Summary: A survey of the job satisfaction of daycare personnel, of factors affecting this, of psychosomatic symptoms and of their satisfaction with life.

Theoretical frame of reference: A practical approach.

Method employed: Questionnaire of 287 randomly selected daycare teachers, children's nurses and daycare assistants from municipal daycare centres in the city of Turku. The results can be applied to other municipal daycare centres in Finnish cities.

Results: Most of the personnel were satisfied with their jobs. As few as 9% were dissatisfied. They were aware, though, of different inconveniences connected with their work, caused by noise, by lack of time and by lack of guidance at work. Most of them felt that they were in good health and half of them were considered healthy. 16% had a number of psychosomatic symptoms, which is less than the Finnish adult population in general. Most of them were satisfied with their lives. Only 10% were not. There was a correlation between job satisfaction and satisfaction with life, and there were fewer psychosomatic symptoms in this group.

* * *

Kiviluoto, H. & T. Parkkinen (1976). *Varhaislapsuuden erilaisten kasvuympäristöjen vaikutus lapsen kehitykseen. Kodin, päivähoiden avioeron ja syntymäpoikkeavuuden vaikutuksista*/The Influence of Different Rearing Environments on the Preschool Child. Concerning the Influence of the Home, the Daycare, Divorces and Deviant Births. Turku: Turun yliopiston psykologian julkaisuja, 21/1976. ISBN 951-641-360-9. In Finnish.

Summary: A survey of the influence of different rearing environments on the cognitive and socio-emotional development of the child.

Theoretical frame of reference: A theoretical and practical (social-political) approach.

Method employed: 156 socially homogenous children aged 5 years and 6 months - 6 years and 3 months were tested psychologically and observed in the testing situations. The children were divided into 5 groups. One had been looked after at home by the mother, one in a daycare centre, one by the grandmother, one consisted of children of divorced parents and the last was a risk-group consisting of children whose birth had been deviant. In addition, the mothers were interviewed.

Results: There were no statistically significant differences in the cognitive or the socio-emotional development of the children looked after either by the mother, in a daycare centre or by the grandmother. The socio-emotional, but not the cognitive development of children of divorced parents, deviated from the others according to both the tests and the mothers. The reasons for the deviations are to be found in family relations and the rearing attitudes and -behaviour of the parents.

* * *

Kiviluoto, H., R. Antila & K. Salo (1981). *Viisivuotiaiden lasten laajennetun terveystarkastuksen ja kehityksen tukemisen kokeilu Turussa*/An Experiment in Turku With Extended Health Control and Developmental Support of 5 year-olds. Turku: Turun yliopisto. Psykologian tutkimuksia, 54/1981. ISBN 951-642-096-6. In Finnish.

Summary: The survey aims to explain how health control of 5 yearolds can be extended to contain an evaluation of the child's development as a whole. This should make it possible to help children, who need to be supported in their development already before school-age.

Theoretical frame of reference: Of a practical, social and political interest.

Method employed: Assessment of the cognitive level and the socioemotional development of 307 children. Questionnaires of and semi-structured interviews with the mothers, about the developmental environment of the child, about her pregnancy, about the birth of the child and about its development during the first year of life.

Results: 70% of the children examined were in good health, but about half of them had minor developmental problems. The development of the boys was more exposed to disturbances, but both sexes had the same quantity of developmental problems. The recommended rehabilitation arrangements; placement in daycare centres and in rehabilitation groups, examination by speech therapists and continuous examinations of the cognitive level, were accepted and used. In a follow-up examination one year later, it turned out that an adjustment regarding development had taken place in 16.8% of the cases with problems or disturbances.

* * *

Korkiakangas, M. (1982). *Vanhempien neuvolan 5-vuotistarkastuksessa esiin tuomat lapsen psyykkisen kehityksen ja kasvatuksen pulmat*/Problems Pointed Out by Parents in Connection With Health Control Concerning the Psychological Development and Rearing of 5 Year-Olds in the Daycare Centre. Helsinki: LKH:n julkaisuja, 12. In Finnish.

Summary: A statement of how the psychological development and the rearing situation of children can be evaluated in connection with the health control of 5 year-olds in the daycare centre. Is part of the project "Evaluation of the Psychological Development Level of Children".

Theoretical frame of reference: A social-political approach.

Method employed: Questionnaire of the parents of 75 children in 3 different places.

Results: The following kinds of problems were experienced by the parents: 43% find that the children become obstinate, if they don't get their way, 37% say, that the children are fastidious about their food, 3% that they were afraid of vaccinations, 23% that they were afraid of ghosts and other figments of the imagination, 20% of what they saw on television and 20% of "something" or of some animals. The sex had no connection with the number of problems mentioned by the parents, but girls were more often afraid of animals. On the other hand, the boys were more often afraid of vaccinations and other measures of caretaking. The boys were more boisterous when they were together with other children, while the girls were more controlling. The educational level of the parents had no connection with the number of problems. In the case of parents with a good knowledge of rearing, the number of problems was "normally" distributed. In the case of parents with little knowledge of rearing, a great number stated that they had many problems and the rest, that they hardly had any problems at all. According to the nursing personnel, about 20% of the children or the families needed continuous support from a psychologist or speech-therapist.

* * *

Kuusela, L. (1984). *Äitien ja näiden viisivuotiaitten lasten peloista, äitien suhtautumisesta lasten pelkoihin ja äitien toimista erilaisissa pelkotilanteissa*/Mothers and the Fears of Their 5-Year-Olds, the Attitudes of the Mothers Towards the Fears of the Children and the Actions of the Mothers in Situations of Fear. Tampere: University of Tampere. Master thesis in psychology. In Finnish.

Summary: A study of the fears of mothers, the fears of their children and of the actions of the mothers in 6 different situations of fear. The connection between the sex of the child and the mother's judgement of the child's character, on the one hand and how often the child experiences fear and of how it reacts to fear situations according to the mother, on the other.

Theoretical frame of reference: Within the framework of general developmental psychology.

Method employed: Questionnaire of and interviews with the mothers in 30 families.

Results: The children's fear was mainly connected with nature and with supernatural things. The fears of the mothers, on the other hand, was connected with social and psychological stress situations and with physical harm and personal security. According to the mothers, children characterised as shy were more often afraid than courageous children. The mothers emphasised that security in the home, the example of the parents, the character of the child, its experience and undeveloped skills, were of importance. The actions of the mothers were edifying or supporting, depending on the situation. In unambiguous situations it was mostly edifying, while supporting actions were applied in fear situations by the shy children. The sex of the child had no connection with the actions of the mothers.

* * *

Lahikainen, A. R. & M. Asikainen (1983). *Äidin kotona hoitamien kaksivuotiaiden sosiaalinen kehitys John Bowlbyn kiintymysteorian kannalta*/The Social Development of 2 Year-Olds Looked After at Home by the Mother On the Basis of John Bowlby's Attachment Theory. Helsinki: University of Helsinki. ISBN 951-45-2872. In Finnish.

Summary: The aims of the survey were 1) to survey the attachment relations of 2 year-olds looked after at home by the mother and the quality of these relations. 2) to look for a connection between the caring attitudes of the mother, the child's relations with her and the socio-emotional well-being of the child.

Theoretical frame of reference: Within the framework of John Bowlby's attachment theory.

Method employed: The sample (100 families) represents families in the area of Helsinki. Questionnaires of both the fathers and the mothers with questions about family relations, division of work in the family, the child's way of showing attachment to the father and to the mother, the social behaviour of the child and behaviour expressing emotional well-being, or the opposite.

Results: The child had several objects of attachment. According to the estimation of the mothers, 83% were primarily attached to the mother, 71% to the father, 24% to brothers and sisters and 4% to grandparents. There were no significant divisions concerning the attachment or quality of the attachment to the father and the mother. However, the type of relations effected the socio-emotional well-being of the child. The most important relation was to the mother and having a secure attachment to the father could not compensate for an insecure relationship with the mother, if she took care of the child at home. The attachment to the parents had no significant connection with the sociability of the child or the relations to children of the same age. This depended mostly on whether the child had sisters and brothers. The rearing attitudes, the sensitivity, cooperation and acceptance of the mother and the security of the attachment, had a direct connection with the socio-emotional well-being of the child. On the other hand, the psychological attention and the acceptance of the mother, mostly effected the security of the attachment. There was a correlation between the security of the attachment and the social-emotional well-being.

* * *

Lahikainen, A. R. & S. Sundqvist (1979). *Kolmevuotiaiden ja sitä nuorempien lasten reaktiot päivähoitoon*/The Reactions of Children Under 4 Years to Kindergarten. Acta Psychiatrica Fennica. ISBN 951-909-032-3. ISSN 0079-7227.

Summary: The aims of the study were to ascertain: 1) To what extent the kindergarten experience is regarded as an event of separation and how the children respond. 2) Types of separation responses. Is separation concerning kindergarten comparable with long periods of separation? 3) Which external aspects of separation are the most influential on the quality and strength of perceived responses?

Theoretical frame of reference: Within the framework of J. Bowlby's attachment theory.

Method employed: A sample of 130 children of age 1-3 years attending municipal kindergarten for 8 hours a day. All the children had attended the kindergarten regularly for a period of 4-6 weeks, while earlier experiences from daycare varied. Questionnaires of the parents and the personnel about the children's behaviour in different social contexts and situations during the day.

Results: The following behaviour patterns were found: 1) Protest against being left behind in the kindergarten. 2) Clinging behaviour towards the mother after returning home. 3) Accusatory behaviour towards the mother, when fetched in the kindergarten. 4) Resentment against going to the kindergarten. 5) Active hostility in the kindergarten. 6) Depression and withdrawal from common activities, peers and the personnel. 7) Attachment towards the personnel. The behaviour patterns were age-dependent.

The youngest children protested most when left behind in the kindergarten. 2-3 year-olds mostly exhibited "accusing" behaviour and fear of the kindergarten was most common among children older than 3 years. The earlier experiences of daycare correlated with the types of behaviour patterns that the children showed in the kindergarten.

* * *

Lasten *kehitystutkimus. Osa 3: Kolmas ikävuosi*/A Study of the Development of the Child. Part 3: The Third Year of Life (1984). Official Statistics of Finland. Special Social Studies, XXXII:102. ISBN 951-46-8560-1. In Finnish.

Summary: The aim of the study is to give information about the influence of the different kinds of childcare on the development of the child. Attention is also drawn to the relations among the members of the family and to the influence of these on the development of the child.

Theoretical frame of reference: Of a general developmental-psychological and social-political outlook.

Method employed: A longitudinal study and visits in the homes of 336 (in the end 315) children in 8 municipalities (half of them cities and the other half rural districts) by a child psychiatrist, who observed the child and the family. Visits by the daycare personnel. The families represented different social groups and different family types.

Results: Daycare: At the age of 3, about half of the children examined were looked after at home by their own parents. 74% of the parents wanted their children to be looked after at home. Concerning the daycare personnel, 59% were of the opinion that it would be desirable if the mother could take care of the child until the age of 3-6. Of the children who were looked after in daycare centres, 73% were in the same daycare centre at the age of 3. Of the private childminders, only 5% were educated, they were also valued lowest. According to the personnel of the daycare centres and the childminders, the cooperation with the parents was good in 68% of the cases. The development and the health of the child: The children who were looked after outside the home, had better moto-functions. The children looked after at home by other persons than the parents, were more social. Children who were looked after at home by their own parents were less noisy and restless than other children. Social stress factors, when being looked after in a daycare centre and parental difficulties correlated with restlessness. The psychological state of the children was estimated to be free of symptoms in 71% of the cases. 9.3% had obvious symptoms. Among these, the children who had changed from one kind of daycare to another, outnumbered the other children. The number of families risking mental problems increased to 23% when the child was 3 years old. Risk factors: The possibilities of minor disturbances were found in 41.2% of the children and of serious ones in 6.9%. According to the parents, the restlessness of the child was clearly connected with factors of social stress.

* * *

Luolaja, J. (1978). *Perheen kommunikaatioilmasto tutkimuksennkehittyminen ja uusi sovellutuskokeilu*/The Communication Climate in the Family. The Development of Climate Research and a New Experiment of Application. Jyväskylä: University of Jyväskylä. Reports from the department of Psychology, 201. ISBN 951-677-978-6. In Finnish.

Summary: Analysis of the basic factors of the climate in families with children. A report on part of the project: Family Way of Life, Parental Awareness of Parenthood and the Social Development of Children.

Theoretical frame of reference: Within the tradition of way of life research.

Method employed: Questionnaire of 212 families with an only child at the age of 6-7, from 7 localities in Finland.

Results: The basic dimensions of the communication climate of the family, are the following: A positive emotionalism and democratic attitude and a negative emotionalism and control. More specific structures also appeared in the factor-analysis: positive emotionalism, control, negative emotionalism, authoritarian aggressiveness and democratic acceptance. Furthermore, it was found that the communication structures of the mothers and fathers on the whole corresponded. The sex of the parents turned out to be a discriminating factor, first and foremost in connection with dimensions of emotionalism in the communication climate of the family. In connection with parental control of the child's behaviour, there were no significant differences between the parents. Looking at differences according to the locality, the dimension of democratic acceptance was most conspicuous, but the differences were not as great as in earlier surveys.

* * *

Luolaja, J. (1978). *Perheen säännöt. Lapsia koskevien sääntöjen, kontrollimenettelyjen ja sääntöjen tärkeyden kuvaus suomalaisissa perheissä*/The Rules of the Family. A Description of the Rules Affecting the Children; About the Importance of Means of Control and Rules in a Finnish Family. Jyväskylä: University of Jyväskylä. Reports from the Department of Psychology, 204. ISBN 951-678-033-4. In Finnish.

Summary: The study aims to describe the rules and means of control in different families and the parents' opinions about the importance of rules. A method is also developed.

Theoretical frame of reference: Within the tradition of way of life research.

Method employed: Interviews with the parents in 212 Finnish families with an only 6 year-old child.

Results: On an average there are 1.7 parental rules per family. Nearly one third of the families could not spontaneously mention any rule or rule-like habit to be followed in the family. The rules mentioned most often, had to do with family's life together. Next were rules concerning health and cleanliness and rules concerning behaviour towards elderly people and people in general. Offences against the rules were usually followed by rebuke or punishment, while neglect of duties usually was met with indifference. The most common means of control was scolding, which. was used in every second family. Every fifth family used only talks and explanations as means of control and every tenth only rebuke and punishment for offences against all kinds of rules. Totally ignoring transgressions did not occur. The rules concerning behaviour towards elderly people and people in general, were considered to be most important. The number of rules depended on the locality, so that in the bigger cities, as well as in remote localities, there were several families, who could not spontaneously mention any rule at all. In every second family the parents had decided upon the rules, in every fourth the parents and the children had agreed upon them. 8% of the parents had appropriated the rules from their own parents. In every fifth of the remote living families, the rules were based on tradition.

* * *

Luolaja, J. (1979). *Vanhempien ja lasten kasvatuksellinen vuorovaikutus*/The Rearing Interaction of Parents and Children. Jyväskylä: University of Jyväskylä. Licentiate Thesis in psychology.

Summary: The aim of the survey was to develop an instrument for the measurement of the climate of the home and rearing. This instrument should be more economic and more homogenous, regarding the content, than earlier instruments with a point of departure in attitudes towards rearing. The values of the family discovered by the new instrument, might later on be compared with less content-characterised facts of rearing. Part of Martti Takalas' project "Family Way of Life, Parental Awareness of Parenthood and Children's Social Development".

Theoretical frame of reference: Social-ecological survey.

Method employed: The empirical instrument of measurement was evaluated on the basis of enquete material on 212 families with one 6 year-old child.

Results: The fundamental dimensions of the communication climate of the family (positive emotionality, democratic attitudes and negative emotionality and aggression) and the more distinctive structures (positive emotionality, control, negative emotionality, authoritarian aggression and democratic acceptance) corresponded with the results of earlier surveys of climate. Futhermore, it was demonstrated, that the structure of the communication climate of the mothers and the fathers, corresponded to a very high degree. The sex of the parents turned out to be a distinctive factor. Dimensions describing the emotionality of communication climate: Concerning dimensions describing the parents' control of the behaviour of children, these showed no significant differences. The biggest differences were found in the dimension of democratic acceptance. The differences between city and rural environment were not as great as in earlier surveys.

* * *

Lyytinen, P. (1976). *Kasvuympäristön yhteyksistä kaksivuotiaiden lasten kielellisiin ja kognitiivisiin taitoihin*/On the Connection Between the Rearing Environment and the Linguistic and Cognitive Skills of 2 Year-Olds. Jyväskylä. University of Jyväskylä, 178. In Finnish.

Summary: A study of the connection between the rearing environments, the behaviour of the mothers and the linguistic and cognitive skills of 2 year-olds. The study has its point of departure in a number of factors that create the background for a favourable interaction: In situations with play activities, the linguistic expressions are altered to correspond to the developmental level of the child, the behaviour of the child is supported, the initiative of the child is responded to, the child is motivated and instructed in its activities and is offered possibilities to examine the environment, to gain experience through activities and learning and to establish secure human relations.

Theoretical frame of reference: Of a Soviet-psychological and social-interactional outlook.

Method employed: Measurements of the child's cognitive and linguistic skills. Filming of the interaction of the mothers' and children's groups in structured tête-a-tête situations. Interviews, questionnaires and a follow-up measurement of the skills of the children after 8 months.

Results: The following factors were connected with the linguistic and cognitive skills of the children. The behaviour of the mother: The code for the linguistic expressions, explanations of how to perform tasks correctly, supporting statements, flexible interaction behaviour and eye contact. The rearing environment: The time that the mother spends daily with the child, explanations of behaviour in daily situations and the quality of the child's toys.

* * *

Makkonen, T. et al. (1981). *Operaatio perhe- isä synnytys*/Operation Family, Father and Delivery. Helsinki. Mannerheimin Lastensuojeluliiton lapsiraportti, A.34. ISBN 951-9311-64-5. In Finnish.

Summary: In the project, the immediate and long lasting effects of a family delivery on the development of the father-child relation in particular, is illuminated. In addition, the effects on the mother-child relation, of intensive birth preparation and the fact that the mother could take care of the child immidiately after the delivery, were examined.

Theoretical frame of reference: An empirical approach.

Method employed: The study is a follow-up study. The sample consisted of 164 families having their first child. The families were interviewed 5 times; when the child was 1 month old, 6 months old and 1, 2 and 3 years old. The parents were divided into 3 groups: 1) Intensive birth preparation, where the father was present at the delivery. 2) Intensive birth preparation, where the father was not present at the delivery. (In both of these groups, the mothers took care of their child immediately after the delivery). 3) The control group received the usual birth preparation, but the father was not present at the delivery and the mother did not take care of the child herself.

Results: According to the results, both the personnel and the parents experienced the family delivery as very positive. The delivery experience of the mother was more positive and less straining. The follow-up study showed that these mothers nursed their children longer and had more positive relations to their children. The fathers who had been present at the delivery, participated more in the care of the child and had more positive attitudes towards the child. The relations between the parents who shared the delivery experience, were better. The family delivery seemed to have a connection with the positive development of the child in general. These parents also seemed to be more sensitive towards the needs of the child and to use less punishment.

* * *

Munter, H. (1985). *Alle kolmevuotiaiden lasten päivähoiden sisällön kehittäminen: Vuosina 1972-1978 suoritetun tutkimuksen lätökohdat, eteneminen ja arviointi*/The Development of Daycare For Children Under 3 Years of Age: Point of departures, Progress and Evaluation of a Survey Carried Out During 1972-1978. Jyväskulä: University of Jyväskylä. Licentiate thesis in psychology. In Finnish.

Summary: The aim of the research project was to study the rearing activities for children younger than 3 years old. The development of the project is described by showing the results and observations ruling the direction of the work, the choice of methods and the basis on which the perception of the rearing arose.

Theoretical frame of reference: Within the theory that development and rearing are mutually connected.

Method employed: Based on existing material and on action research, where the fundamental problems of daycare work and the lines of direction for activities, have been discussed with the personnel for one year.

Results: The development of the work in the daycare centre implies a long-range co-ordinated collaboration between the personnel and the researchers. The efforts were most successful when the initiative for renewal was taken by the personnel. A practical result of the project was that one of the daycare centres was especially activated to develop its activities in an original way. The material gathered is used as teaching material in the education of nursery teachers and as the basis of the instructions for the rearing work of the daycare.

* * *

Niemelä, P., M.-L. Mäki & K. Laaksonen (1982). *Äitiyteen valmentavien keskusteluryhmien merkitys. Ensimmäisen raskauden aikana ja lapsen syntymän jälkeen toimivien keskusteluryhmien vaikutus raskauden ja äitiyden kokemiseen*/The Importance of Discussion Groups Preparing for Motherhood. How Does Attending Discussion Groups During the First Pregnancy and After Delivery Influence the Experience of Pregnancy and Motherhood? Turku: Turun yliopisto. Psykologian tutkimuksia, 56. ISBN 951-642-120-2, ISSN 035-8741. In Finnish.

Summary: The study is part of the project "Naisen eläm n käännekohdat (Turning Points in the Life of a Woman). The importance of attending discussion groups during the pregnancy and after the delivery for the experience of motherhood and for changes in the marriage, was evaluated.

Theoretical frame of reference: The phase of becoming a family is analysed as being a crisis in identity development. Psychodynamic and systems-theoretical accentuation.

Method employed: A test group consisting of 28 women attending discussion groups, during their first pregnancy and a control group of 35 women, who did not attend any groups. Interviews 1 month before and 3 month after the delivery. The delivery was judged by midwives. The interviews contained observations about the breast feeding.

Results: The mothers in the test group accepted and worked more often on their feelings concerning motherhood. They experienced uncertainty more often, were more often ready to ask for support and they experienced their difficulties on a psychological level. They had fewer difficulties delivering and they experienced the delivery more positively. The relationship between the spouses became closer in the test group.

* * *

Belonging to the same project:

Niemelä, P. & R. Pylkäs (1982). *Äitiyteen valmentavien keskusteluryhmien puheenaiheet. Ensimmäisen raskauden aikana ja lapsen syntymän jälkeen toimivien keskusteluryhmien puheenaiheet erityyppisissä ryhmissä sekäeri ryhmäkerroilla*/Topics in Groups Preparing for Motherhood. Topics in Different Types of Groups Functioning During the First Pregnancy, After the Delivery and in Different Group Get-togethers. Turku: Turun yliopisto. Psykologian tutkimuksia, 61. ISBN 951-642-226-8. In Finnish.

Results: All of the groups talked most about the delivery, the child and the relationship to the spouse. The groups of mothers talked more about feelings in connection with the pregnancy and the delivery and about ambivalent feelings towards the child and childcare, which the groups of couples only did after the delivery.

* * *

Nummenmaa, A.-R., M. Asonen, M. Turpeinen, A. Talvinen & E. Äkäslompolo (1983). *Perheen toiminnan kokonaisrakenne kehitysvaihemuutoksen kuvaajana. Tutkimus ensimmäisen ja toisen lapsen syntymisen vaikutuksesta perheen jokapäiväiseen elämään*/The Total Structure of the Activities of a Family, Seen as a Delineation of a Change of Developmental Phases. A Study of How the Births of the

First and the Second Child Influence the Daily Life of the Family. Tampere: University of Tampere. Reports from the Department of psychology, 133. ISBN 951-44-1484-5. In Finnish.

Summary: The aim of the study is to test how analysis of the family's activity patterns adapts to the description of changes of short time intervals, by elucidating the changes happening in everyday life and the activities of a family, when a new family member is born.

Theoretical frame of reference: An environmental-psychological theory.

Method employed: A two step questionnaire of the spouses in families in Tammerfors, expecting their first or second child. The first questionnaire was completed 2-3 months before the child was born and involved 41 couples and one mother expecting their first child, and 35 couples and 3 mothers expecting their second child. The second questionnaire involved 28 and 30 couples, respectively.

Results: The biggest changes occurred in the field of housework; the work of the mothers increased. The families and especially those who, before the child was born, had a relatively equal distribution of work, returned to a more traditional pattern. For the mothers, the birth of the child meant an obvious decrease in leisure activities. 46% of the mothers and 36% of the fathers expecting their first child and 54% of the mothers expecting their second child, had realistic expectations. The mothers expecting their second child, had more realistic expectations concerning housework and childcare than mothers expecting their first child. The participation of the fathers in housework was estimated too high by both spouses expecting their first child and the extent of the housework was underestimated by the mothers in this group. According to 43% of the mothers and 54% of the fathers, their relationship had improved after the birth of the child and according to 50% of the mothers and 39% of the fathers, it had deteriorated.

* * *

Nupponen, R. & L. Simonen (1983). *Kodinhoitajan tehostettu perhetyö. Valtakunnallisen kokeilun loppuraportti*/Project for the Development of the Professional and Practical Skills of Municipal Home Helpers in Long-Term Work. A Description and Evaluation of a Real-life Experiment in Finland 1976-1981. Helsinki: Mannerheimin Lastensuojeluliiton Lapsiraportti A, 41. ISBN 951-9311-90-4. Issn 0359-1808. In Finnish. With an English Summary.

Summary: The aim was to develop a municipal home help and to adapt the professional and practical skills of the home helpers, to the circumstances and problems of families with children in present-day society. The project also aimed to coordinate the municipal home help services with other social and health services, directed towards families with children.

Theoretical frame of reference: Of a social-political interest.

Method employed: A field experiment involving 100 home helpers and professionals, working in 70 families with children, for 2-3 days a week. The working periods varied from a few weeks to more than a year. The research material comprises the individual reports made every year by the participants, each of whom was also interviewed and questionnaired of the client families. During the field experiment, selected findings from this material were included in supervision and training. There was a short period of training in the beginning, as well as during the experiment. Furthermore, the home helpers were guided and supervised regulary.

Results: A more systematic approach to the work, was the most important principle. The home helpers in particular, but also the experts involved in guidance and supervision, succeeded in applying a more systematic plan of action in their work. Likewise, another important principle, teamwork, was increased. The systematic approach and the teamwork were also applied, when selecting the families and organising the administration of the long-term intensive work.

* * *

Säntti, R. & U. Husa (1986). *Lasten hoito*/Child Care. *Kotityö-tutkimus, osa XI*/Housework Study, part XI. Helsinki: Official Statistics of Finland. Special Social Studies, XXXXII (B II). ISBN 951-46-6425-6, ISSN 0071-5336. In Finnish. With a Summary in English.

Summary: The report is part of a research project on the value of unpaid housework. The purpose of this part of the study was to find out, in what types of families the preschool children were looked after in the home, in what types they were looked after outside the home and for how long they were in daycare. Other questions investigated were the family's need of contemporary care and to what extent preschool children participated in supervised play and similar activities arranged away from home.

Theoretical frame of reference: Of a social-political interest.

Method employed: A sample consisting of 364 families with preschool children. Background information was gathered through interviews, while time-use diaries, among other things, were used to collect data on the time spent on childcare.

Results: The proportion of families with at least one preschool child, who was looked after outside the home, came to 42%. The number of children was slightly higher on an average, in families where the child was looked after in the home. In 54% of the families with only one child, the child was cared for in the home. 73% of the families, where the mother had a job during the day, were dependent on care arrangements outside the home; mostly more than 30 hours a week. About half of the 6 year-olds were looked after for a maximum of 20 hours a week outside the home. The incidence of part-time childcare was considerably lower in other age groups. About half of the families used temporary childcare, most of them less than 5 hours a month. 27% of the families had children, who participated in supervised play and similar activities, outside the home. The average time of active childcare in the family was 4.1 hours a day. This increased with the number of children. The age of the youngest child, clearly effected the time used. The least time spent on childcare was in families were the mother had a job.

* * *

Taskinen, S. & A. Tirkkonen (1984). *Perhekasvatuksen kehittäminen päiväkotien ja kasvatusneuvoloiden yhteistyönä/*Development of Family Rearing as a Cooperation Between the Daycare Centres and the Guidance Offices for Rearing Questions. Helsinki: Sosiaalihallituksen julkaisuja, 8. ISBN 951-46-8624-1. In Finnish.

Summary: The aim of the project was to develop possibilities for the organisation of a councelling activity for rearing questions in the daycare centres. The period of examination was 1982-1984. During the first phase, the personnel participating in the project was choosen and during the second phase, spring 1984, the experiment was carried out.

Theoretical frame of reference: A social-political approach.

Method employed: A preliminary survey, where small-group activities and rearing guidance at 4 colleges for the education of daycare personnel, were studied. An adviser education for the personnel at the guidance offices was established. The experiments in the daycare centres included the following phases: The parents were invited to a talk with the personnel at the beginning of the period. In the autumn the personnel paid visits to all of the homes. Instead of the usual parents' evenings, meetings were arranged, where rearing questions were discussed with small groups of parents. The parents were given written material about rearing. After a year, the experiment was evaluated by 298 families.

Results: 88% of the parents considered the talk with the personnel to be very, or quite useful. 87% considered the visit in the home to be quite useful. The meetings in small groups were considered useful by 46% of the parents and the written material by 75%. The children had been eagerly waiting for the home visits and the parents considered them to be important. 86% of parents, who had earlier experience with daycare centres, considered the established cooperation to be better than the usual forms of co-operation. 87% had expectations regarding the daycare centre and 22% regarding the guidance offices concerning rearing questions. The personnel considered the experiment to be stressing but fruitful. 93% gave priority to this kind of cooperation. 61% of the personnel and all of the advisers at the guidance offices considered the establishment of guidance in rearing questions in the daycare centres to be meaningful and possible.

* * *

Vehviläinen, M.R. (1982). *Sukupuoliroolit lasten päiväkodeissa*/Sex Roles in Daycare Centres. 2. rev. ed. Helsinki: Valtioneuvoston kanslian julkaisuja, 8. ISBN 951-859-205-5. In Finnish.

Summary: A statement of how children's sex roles and attitudes towards these, are influenced in daycare centres for 3-6 year-old children and of how the prevailing sex roles prevent equality between the sexes.

Theoretical frame of reference: Theories of sex roles as a result of learning. Cognitive developmental theory.

Method employed: Unstructured participant observations in 3 municipal and 1 private daycare centre in Helsinki. The daycare centres were selected, so that they represented the different conditions in the city, in the best way possible.

Results: The traditional sex roles are supported in the daycare centres, among other things, through role play, singing and gymnastics, books and pictures. Obedience is the message in several fairy-tales. This prevents criticism against the prevailing system. The personnel consists mainly of women. Division of the children into groups according to sex, occurs when playing and eating. The girls are eager assistants, while the boys are punished more often and are more often aggressive than the girls. The form that punishing a boy might take, would be to place him among the girls. The girls take the initiative to be tender more often than the boys.

YOUNG CHILDREN'S CULTURAL CONDITIONS

Eräsaari, L. (1979). *Lastenkirjallisuus ja sosialisaatio. Tutkimus lastenkirjallisuudesta sosialisaatioagentuurina suomalaisen (esikouluikäisten) lastenkirjallisuuden valossa*/Children's Literature and Socialisation. A Study of Children's Literature as a Factor of Socialisation in the Light of Finnish Children's Literature (for Children of Preschool Age). Tampere: Yhteiskuntatieden tutkimuslaitos. Tampereen yliopisto, E 10. ISBN 951-44-0814-4.

Summary: A study of children's literature, of its historical frame and of its function in the process of socialisation. A contentual analysis of existing knowledge about society in children's literature.

Theoretical frame of reference: George Lukás' literature studies of the peculiarities of literature. The conception of character mask (Klaus Ottomeyer).

Method employed: The material consists of 30 children's books, published in Finland during 1969-1975. Methods from the traditional empirical sociology of literature and more free interpretations with Lukás as a model.

Results: Central factors influencing the socialisation of children in our time, are the sharp separation of the life sphere, the relative independence during childhood and the poverty in everyday life. Of these, only the last mentioned has been consciously treated in the books. The relative independence of childhood, is reflected in the way that the books to a higher degree are child-concentrated. That children's lives are restricted to leisure time and consumption is reflected in the one-sided economic structure. Children's literature is true to its historical background and often lacks a societal attitude. The different traditions within Finnish children's literature, seem to be based on different perceptions of our children: the religious tradition based on a religious perception, the Finnish-Swedish and the liberal-individual. It was only in the late 1960s that the Finnish children's literature left the traditional perception of the child behind.

* * *

Hälinen, K. (1981). *Huoltajien käsityksiä 3-6-vuotiaiden lasten uskontokasvatuksesta päiväkodissa tarkasteltuna Päivähoidon kasvatustavoitekomitean mietinnön (1980:32) sitä koskevien esitysten näkökulmasta*/The Custody Holders' Opinion of the Religious Instruction of 3-6 Year-Old Children in Daycare Centres, Considered From the Angle of the Recommendations of the Commitee of Rearing Aims of Daycare Centres (1980:31). Helsinki: Helsingin yliopiston kasvatustieteen laitoksen tutkimuksia, 92. ISBN 951-45-2351-2. In Finnish.

Summary: A study of parents' opinions on how basic material for religious instruction ought to be formed.

Theoretical frame of reference: Pedagogical orientated.

Method employed: Questionnaire of 431 mothers and 274 fathers - representative of the users of the daycare services.

Results: The majority of the parents were of the opinion, that because of questions from the children, it is not possible to avoid religious elements in the programme of the daycare centres. The majority of the parents wanted the daycare centres to be engaged in the traditional christian culture. About half of them wanted the instruction to be regular. Only about 20% of the parents not belonging to the church, were opposed to any kind of religious instruction. The mothers were somewhat more positive than the fathers. Mainly, the parents valued the children's feelings of security, in connection with religious questions.

* * *

Kuosmanen, S. (1981). *Taide päiväkotien toiminnassa. Valtakunnallinen selvitys päiväkotien taidekasvatustoiminnasta ja -välineistöstä*/Art as Part of the Activities of the Daycare Centre. A Nationwide Committee Work Concerning the Daycare Centres' Rearing Activities and

Rearing Tools Regarding Art. Helsinki: Mannerheimin lastensuo-
jeluliiho. ISBN 915-9311-52-1. In Finnish.

Summary: Part of an experiment with the purpose of examining the
possibilities of the daycare centres to increase the cultural medi-
ation aimed at children in daycare centres. A review of the material and educational resources for mediating literature, visual
art, music and toy theatre for children of preschool age in the
daycare centres.

Theoretical frame of reference: A practical, pedagogical and social
political approach.

Method employed: Two questionnaires. The first concerning music,
was sent to 55 daycare centres and the other concerning literature, visual art and toy theatre, was sent to 100 daycare centres.
A statistical preparation.

Results: All the daycare centres had apparatus for listening to music,
but no taping facilities. Only every second daycare institution
had a piano and every fourth lacked instruments for accompani-
ment. One of the daycare centres had enough rythmic musical
instruments. Half of them were fairly well equipped with musical
instruments and the other half were scarcely equipped. There
were several reasons for the few and one-sidedness of the activities. Among other things, educational difficulties, but also the
large number of children in the groups and the lack of localities
were a hindrance. Quite a lot of books were read; there is an
average of 2-3 books per child. The selection of books is good.
Every second centre subscribes to a magazine and all use library
books on occasion. The toy theatre is an everyday activity, but
seldom in a way that introduces the children to visual art. The
most common activities that the child can carry out on its own,
are drawing, colouring with crayons, modelling and playing with
toy bricks, the personnel's lack of knowledge and the lack of
localities are a hindrance. The most common materials are present
in a sufficient quantity. Natural materials, such as wood and clay
are scarce. The aims of the daycare centres seldom concern art
and visits to art museums are rare.

Socialization of Young Children in the Nordic Countries

* * *

Kytömäki, J. (1983). *Palautetutkimus television pienten lasten ohjelmista.* *Mielenkiinnon pysyminen, pitäminen, keskustelun syntyminen, vanhempien arviot, TV l:n lastenohjelmien lähetysajat sekä vanhempien terveisiä lastenohjelmien tekijöille ja niistä päättä ville/*A Feedback Survey of Children's Television. How the Interest is Maintained, What the Children Think of the Programmes, How the Parents Value the Programmes. Whether a Discussion Arises, the Transmitting Hours in TV 1 and Statements From the Parents to the Hosts of the Children's Programmes and to Those Who Decide About the Programmes. Helsinki: Oy. Yleistradio Ab. Suunnittelu- ja tutkimusosasto. Sarja B 1. ISBN 951-43-0253-2. ISSN 0357-5179. In Finnish.

Summary: An attempt to answer the following kinds of questions: How do the different children's programmes work? How are they valued? What is the influence of the children's programmes on everyday life.

Theoretical frame of reference: A survey of an empirical descriptive outlook.

Method employed: A questionnaire and an observation, dairy completed by parents of a representative sample of 572 Finnish speaking 3-8 year-old children.

Results: 66% of the children had been concentrating on the programmes. The girls were usually more concentrated than the boys. Exceptions from this were an item with the clown Hermanni and animated cartoons. The 5 year-olds were the most intensive viewers and the 8 year-olds, the least intensive. Well over half of the children liked the programmes showed during the week examined. The programmes mentioned above were also the most popular. The girls liked the programmes better than the boys did. 10-30% of the children had discussed the programmes. The different programmes were given points between 6.92 and 8.96 by the parents on a scale between 4 and 10.

Malkavaara, V. (1983). *Uskontokasvatuksen asema pävähoidon kasvatustavoitteiden määrittelyssä vuosina 1974-1980*/The Position of Religious Education, When Defining the Rearing Aims of the Daycare During the Years 1974-1980. Helsinki: Helsingin yliopiston käytännöllisen teologian laitos. Uskontopedagogiikan julkaisuja, B 10. ISBN 951-45-2899-9. In Finnish.

Summary: The position of religious education compared to ethical rearing during the years when the nationwide aims for the daycare were defined.

Theoretical frame of reference: A historical survey of the position of religious education in the Finnish kindergarten tradition.

Method employed: A reading of the preparatory memorandum of rearing aims of the daycare, prepared by a working group appointed by the social government (1974), the final report by the Parlamenty Committee for the Rearing aims of Daycare (1980) and reports, statements and other documents published between 1974-1980.

Results: During this period, a change of society was ascertained, according to which, rearing in the daycare centres was defined pluralistically and with a point of departure in the tradition of culture. From being part of the ethical rearing in the preparatory memorandum, religious education in the final report was transformed into being a separate field on the same level as ethical rearing. Some ethical principles of a religious kind were detached from their christian context and transferred into the ethical field. Religious education is defined in such a way, that it does not necessitate the sorting of the children into different groups.

* * *

Myllymäki, T. (1983). *Esikasvatusikäisten elämänkysymykset. 4-6 -vuotiaiden päiväkerho- ja päiväkotilasten kokemuksia ja käsityksiä ilosta ja surusta ja uskonnolisuuden yhteys näihin skä lasten van-*

Socialization of Young Children in the Nordic Countries

hempien ja päivähoidon opettajien kasvatusasenteet ja uskonnol-lisuus/Matters of Importance for Children of Preschool Age. Experiences and Perceptions of Joy and Grief Among Children in Daycare Centres and in the Clubs of the Parishes, the Connections of Piety to These Rearing Attitudes and the Piety of the Children's Parents and of the Teachers in the Daycare Centres. Helsinki: University of Helsinki. Master thesis in pedagogical religion. In Finnish.

Summary: Part of a project examining piety and ethical understanding of children in the clubs of the parishes and the daycare centres.

Theoretical frame of reference: Cognitive psychology and religious psychology.

Method employed: Picture interviews, consisting of 12 black-white pictures and 165 questions with 319 children and a questionnaire of 29 teachers and 281 parents.

Results: The daycare pedagogues appreciate the humanitarian values in christian rearing and the pedagogues in the clubs, the christian values. The mothers want their children to be brought up in a christian way. The most religious mothers want their children to relate to religious questions in the same way as they do. To the children, leisure time, positive events and matters attached to the home and friends of the same age, are matters of pleasure. The children do not like to be teased, to quarrel, or not to have it their own way. Grief is often caused by a sad event, a quarrel, or by somebody being scolded. Some children ponder over sad religious matters, but the religious attitudes of the children are by and large, positive. The different components of piety, are connected with the children's ideas and experiences of joy and grief and with variables of social background.

* * *

Nummenmaa, T., K. Ruuhilehto, & M. Syvänen (1975). *Traffic Education Programme for Preschool Children and Children Starting School*. Helsinki: Reports from Liikenneturva, Central Organization for Traffic Safety in Finland, 17. In English.

Summary: The first section of the report deals with an experiment in which the instruction programme, implemented by parents and teachers, was tested in practice. At the end of the section, some aspects noticed in the experiment about arranging traffic education for children of preschool age and children starting school, are presented.

Theoretical frame of reference: A practical approach.

Method employed: 64 6 year-olds from the half-day departments of 3 kindergartens located in the centre of Tampere, where teachers and parents were chosen as test persons. 10 different situations were trained under the supervision of the parents, after the children had seen slides of the situations. The parents recorded the times, they instructed their children in a training diary. After a four week training period the experiment was evaluated by the parents.

Results: 50 children had received traffic instruction from their parents. The average hours of training were about 88 per child. The use of pedestrian crossings and other actions linked with crossing the street, were trained most. 67% of the children were mainly instructed by their mothers. Normally one training pass lasted for about 15 minutes. The 3 most important training subjects expressed by the parents were pedestrian crossings and their use (mentioned 37 times), looking to the side and behind (26 times) and stopping (21 times). According to the 5 instructors, the most difficult subjects to train were aspects related to looking out for automobiles, assessment of distances and vehicles and watching automobiles approaching from all four directions. 3 parents thought that there had been no significant changes in the skills of the children. The greatest changes noticed, concerned pedestrian crossings (mentioned 18 times), looking to the side and behind (12 times) and stopping (9 times) and least changes, in walking on the sidewalk (15 times).

* * *

Partanen, T. (1983). *Eriikäisten sisarusten kielellinen vuorovaiku-tus*/Linguistic Interaction Between Brothers and Sisters of Different Ages. Tampere: University of Tampere. Master thesis in psychology. In Finnish.

Summary: A statement of the nature of the linguistic interaction between children, who are learning to speak and their older sisters and brothers and how the age differences are reflected in this interaction.

Theoretical frame of reference: A practical approach.

Method employed: Observation of 20 pairs of children in groups: one group of pairs with a 2 year-old and a 4 year-old brother or sister and the other, of a 2 year-old and a 6 year-old brother or sister.The two other groups consisted of pairs of friends: One, of the 4 year-old brothers and sisters and their friends and the other of the 6 year-old brother and sisters and their friends. The examination took place in 2 daycare centres in Tammerfors. Each pair was observed for 55 minutes. Tape recordings were made of the talks.

Results: In the interaction with a younger brother or sister, the 4 year-olds simplified their language more than the 6 years-olds did. Statistically significant differences were only found in the length of the sentences. Both 4 year-olds and 6 year-olds used a more simplified language, among other things shorter expressions, in interaction with their smaller brothers and sisters than in interaction with their friends. The talking passages were also shorter. Both the 4 year-olds and the 6 year-olds were linguistically more active, in that they asked more questions of their brothers and sisters, than of their friends. However, the 6 year-olds were linguistically more active, in that they asked their smaller brothers and sisters questions more often and in that they corrected and instructed them more often.

* * *

Pulkkinen, L. et al. (1980). *Myönteisen sosiaalisen käyttäytymisen varhaiskehitys*/Early Development of a Positive Social Behaviour. Jyväskylä: University of Jyväskylä. Reports from the Department of Psychology, 230.

Summary: An analysis of the occurrence of positive social behaviour before school age, an examination of different age dependent aspects of social behaviour, of the connection between different traits of social behaviour and their connection with intellectual behaviour, social maturity and the dynamic structure of the personality.

Theoretical frame of reference: An empirical approach.

Method employed: Linguistic and non-linguistic tests, interviews, the assessment of teachers, the observation and assessment by the researchers of behaviour and tests of cognitive and social developmental level and of the dynamic structure of the personality. The sample consisted of 94 4-6 year-olds.

Results: Social behaviour increases with age. At the age of 5, there is a deviation from the linear development of behaviour. In most of the tests, there is a positive correlation between positive social behaviour and level of linguistic development and a negative correlation between linguistic development and aggressivity. Positive social behaviour seems to be accumulated by children who are constructive, who try to manage difficult situations in an active and sensible way, who negotiate and try to be fair.

* * *

Pölkki, P. (1976). *Kuusivuotiaiden sosiaaliset perustaidot ja niiden yhteydet kognitiiviseen tasoon ja tilannetekijöihin*/The Basic Social Skills of 6 Year-Olds and Their Connection With Cognitive Level and Situation. Jyväskylä: University of Jyvskylä. Reports from the Department of Psychology, 180. ISBN 951-677-695-7. In Finnish.

Summary: The study aims at developing a system by which children's linguistic and non-linguistic interaction can be described. Besides the connection between the cognitive level of the 6 year-old child, on the one hand and the varying degree of complexity of basic social skills, on the other, the connection between different functions of egocentric speech, cognitive level and situation and social skills, is studied.

Theoretical frame of reference: Piaget's cognitive developmental theory and the dialectic marxist-based developmental psychology, with its point of departure in Vygotsky.

Method employed: In the first phase, an analysis of the social skills and egocentric speech of 20 6 year-olds and 20 7 year-olds was undertaken. In the second phase, films with 24 girls who know each other and of an average age of 6-8 years, were made. The girls were divided into two groups depending on their cognitive level; in one situation with a girl from the same group and in another with a girl from the other group. The functions of the language and of the social and egocentric behaviour were analysed, as well as of the consequences of actions with specifications of the relevance of the answers of the friends.

Results: Some simple forms of social skills (like talking in turn, giving relevant answers and asking questions) obviously lacked correlation with the cognitive level. Communication was impeded by the uneven cognitive levels. The forms of interaction were strongly dependent on the situation. The pairs, where both girls were on the same higher cognitive level, mastered the synchronising of the length of the talks, the orientations towards the other partner and the basic social functions of the language better, than the other pairs. The quality of the egocentric speech was connected with both the situation and the activity, but not with the cognitive level. Social episodes took place more often with pairs on the same cognitive level.

* * *

Rasinaho, A.-L. (1978). *Päiväkotien alle kolmevuotiaiden lasten opetus- ja toimintatuokioden kokeilu*/An Experiment in Daycare Centres With Periods of Learning and Activities Involving Children

Younger Than 3 Years of Age. Jyväskylä. University of Jyväskylä. Reports from the Department of Psychology, 207. ISBN 951-678-072-5. In Finnish.

Summary: Part of a study initiated by the Finnish Social Department in 1972, aimed at effecting a qualitative development in childcare, rearing and educational activities in the daycare.

Theoretical frame of reference: A practical approach.

Method employed: 10 periods of learning and activities for groups of infants (an average of 5 children), for young children (an average of 4 children) and for bigger children (an average of 4 children) in 3 daycare centres, were observed and evaluated by researchers. The periods of the observation of the infants lasted, on average 6 minutes, of the young children, 12 minutes, and of the bigger children, 13.5 minutes.

Results: Periods of teaching and activities turned out to be adaptable to the daily programme of children younger than 3. Teaching methods: Concerning infants, teaching is equal to interaction with an adult. The child becomes familiar with the environment by means of adult guidance. Young children learn through imitation, through talks with adults and through observations. Concerning the bigger children, group interaction is of great importance. The planning and the leader: When the leader has a complete programme for the period, she can foresee the course of it and can control the group situation. Relations between teaching and play: The children usually changed the periods into play, or would have liked to change the learning elements into play. They do not adapt what is learned very quickly, if they are not given the possibility to repeat it in their play. Ending of the periods: The children are not given signs to end the periods themselves.

* * *

Rasku-Puttonen, H. (1982). *Dyadic Verbal and Nonverbal Communication Between Parent and Child in Families With Different Educational Backgrounds.* Jyväskylä: University of Jyväskylä. Psykologian laitoksen julkaisuja. ISBN 951-678-741-x. ISSN 0357-167x. In English.

Summary: The aim of the study was to examine, whether there are difficulties in the verbal or non-verbal communication style of different social groups.

Theoretical frame of reference: An empirical approach.

Method employed: A sample of 40 mothers and fathers and their 7 year-old child were divided into groups. The educational levels of the parents were compared and differences between the mother-child and the father-child communication, were looked for.

Results: There were no significant differences between higher and lower educational groups, with respect to non-verbal communication. Also, there was a high degree of similarity between the linguistic aspects of speech. There were differences, however, between educational level regarding aspects of the planning of speech, the control of the participation of the child and the control of social interaction. Only a few differences existed between the communication of the fathers and mothers and between boys and girls. Children with parents belonging to groups of a higher educational level, mastered the morphological forms better than children with parents of a lower educational level. Better educated parents gave hints more regularly during communication, were more explicit in teaching rules and controlled that the children followed the rules. Nevertheless, on the whole, parents of a lower educational level were more successful in controlling the child's behaviour, than the educated groups.

* * *

Ruoppila, I. & M. Korkiakangas (1975). *Esikoulun, lastentarhan ja kodin vaikutus lasten kehitykseen II. Vaikutuksia koskevat tulokset*/The Influence of the Preschool, the Kindergarten and the Home on the Social Development of Children II. Results Concerning the Effects.

Jyväskylä: University of Jyväskylä. Reports from the Department of Psychology. ISBN 951-677-578-0. In Finnish.

Summary: An experiment of establishing a preschool for 6 year-olds supported by the Preschool Committee, during the school year 1971-1972. The aim was to develop methods for measuring the achieved pedagogical aims of the preschool and for evaluating the influence that preschool has on the motoric, the cognitive and the socio-emotional development of children. It was also examined, whether the preschool had an equalising influence on the children and whether the time spent in preschool, was of importance for the effects.

Theoretical frame of reference: General developmental psychology.

Method employed: 251 6 year-olds from cities and municipalities, of whom 119 went to preschool for 20 hours per week and 32, for 6 hours per week. 54 went to kindergarten and 54 were looked after in the home. Two measurements with an interval of 4-5 months, of the psycho-motoric and physical condition, the cognitive and the socio-emotional development of the children. Individual tests, group observations and assessments of the teachers. Periods of teaching with different themes.

Results: Both in the cities and in the municipalities, the preschool children were developed better motorically and they had a richer vocabulary in the second measurement. Also, concerning the formation of conception, a development had taken place. On the other hand, their ability to cooperate had decreased and according to the teachers, also the social adaptation. In some cases, preschool education has different effects in cities, than in municipalities. A depreciation had taken place in the self-perception of the kindergarten children and of the preschool children living in cities. Concerning the variables of cognitive development, no differences between the groups occurred, but the kindergarten children seemed to have improved more with regard to creative activites, than the kindergarten children and the "home children". The preschool promoted the children's curiousity and criticism . It seemed that a shorter period spent in preschool had better effects than a longer period.

* * *

Sauvala, A, & H. Robinson (1985). *Päivähoidon kasvatustavoitteiden arvostaminen ja toteutuminen Suomessa ja Yhdysvalloissa 1985*/Evaluation and Realisation of Rearing Aims in Finland and the United States of America 1985. Helsinki. ISBN 951-46-8804-x. In Finnish.

Summary: Part of the rearing aim project, which includes all levels of education. The purpose of the study, is to examine the evaluation and realisation of rearing aims of kindergarten teachers and parents in Finland and the USA.

Theoretical frame of Reference: An empirical approach.

Method employed: In Finland, the examination took place in 13 day-care centres, representing the whole country. 14 kindergarten teachers assessed 252 children. 208 parents made the same assessment as the teachers did. The evaluation of different aims made by 63 teachers and 112 parents, constitutes a part-sample. The evaluation was carried out according to the 5-step-Likert-scale.

Results: Generally, the rearing aims are highly estimated. All of the kindergarten teachers agreed upon 22 aims out of 50 and the parents, on 14 aims. The aims concerning personality and ethical-social matters, were estimated the highest. In Finland the parents and the teachers agreed upon the following aims: To help each other, responsibility, to follow common goals and friendship. The aims estimated to have been fulfilled the best, were the personality development and international aims and to be fulfilled the least were, esthetics, health and nationalism. The greatest differences between Finland and USA were: The national aim was realised to a higher degree in USA. The ethical aims were highly estimated and fulfilled in Finland, while in USA, they were among the least fulfilled. The relations of the parents and the teachers to the aims, were different. The former estimated generally smaller aims higher and estimated them to be easier to fulfil, than the teachers did. Sex, civil status, work, age and education played no role in the explanation of differences concerning aims.

* * *

Seitamo, L. (1982). *Kognitiivinen kehitys arktisessa kulttuurissa. Kolttasaamelaisten ja pohjoissuomalaisten lasten kehitystä vertaileva tutkimus ekologisen psykologian ja kaksikulttuurisuuden viitekehyksessä*/Cognitive Development in an Arctic Culture. A Comparative Survey of the Development of Lapish and North Finnish Children Within a Frame of Ecological Psychology and of Belonging to Two Cultures. Jyväskylä: University of Jyväskylä. Department of Psychology. Licentiate thesis. In Finnish.

Summary: A survey of the cognitive development and school progress of children in two Lapish and two North Finnish cities.

Theoretical frame of reference: Earlier surveys of cognitive development, with a point of departure in comparative ecological psychology and in studies of belonging to two cultures and of bilingualism.

Method employed: Test of cognitive development, non-linguistic test of ability of observation and analysis of roles within the culture.

Results: Cognitive adaption to changes within the culture, is a question of the degree of the culture group's development towards the culture of the majority group. If the compulsory school attendence is outgoing from a foreign culture and language, school motivation is low and so is progress in school. Initially, the boys' mastery of the language is poorer than the girls' and this accords with the boys' generally poorer progress in school. In one of the Lapish villages, the structure of economic life has led to perplexity on the part of the fathers and to an accentuating of the role of the mother. The mothers are pushing their daughters into the Finnish society and an acculturation, also in the field of cognitive adaption. Among the North Finnish children, the dominance of the men supported the development of the boys.

* * *

Setälä, M.-L. (1976). *Aikuinen lasten leikkikulttuurin välittäjänä; ulkoleikkien ohjaamisen kokeilu 5-6-vuotiailla*/The Adult as an Intermediary in Children's Play Culture; An Experiment of Instruction in 5-6 Year-Olds Playing Outside. Tampere: University of Tampere. Reports from the Department of Psychology, 101. ISBN 951-44-0459-9. In Finnish.

Summary: A study of whether it is possible for an adult to intermediate to children's play culture through an examination whether an adult, by instructing children in their play, can transfer new forms of performing to the activities.

Theoretical frame of reference: The conditions of children's play and activities, is seen from the perspective of total collective activities.

Method employed: An experiment of instructing children's play in 2 yards (100 children aged 5-7) in the quarter, Hervanta, in Tammerfors. A control yard (60 children), where no instruction was given. Background data was gathered through interviews with 49 of the first citizens in the area. Observation of the games before and after the instruction period.

Results: After the experimental instruction, the children played more than before. During the period of instruction, rule games dominated. The relative frequency of different kinds of games was maintained in the test yards, while the number of rule games decreased in the control yards. Of the 28 and 33 games respectively learned in the experimental period, the children still knew 4 and 12 games respectively at the time of observation. However, the children only played them when the observer was present. The children's spontaneous games were not influenced by the experimental instruction. Change in the games depended on seasonal changes.

ICELANDIC BIBLIOGRAPHY

YOUNG CHILDREN'S CONDITIONS

Björnsson, S., W. Edelstein & K. Kreppner (1977). *Explorations in Social Inequality. Stratification Dynamics in Social and Individual Development in Iceland.* Berlin: Max-Planck-Institut für Bildungsforschung, Studien und Berichte, 38. ISBN 3-12-98242 0-0. GW ISSN 0076-5627. In English.

Summary: A study of facets of a developing system of social inequality that influence the growing individual in Iceland. The objective was to scale social class in Iceland and explore class-related structures, in particular the differential impact of social class on the child rearing patterns of parents, level of cognitive functioning, educational achievement, and mental health. These latter were taken to be prelimininary indicators of cognitive competence and personality functioning.

Theoretical frame of reference: A cross-sectional analysis within Bronfenbrenners theory of "Ecologies of human development".

Method employed: Interviews with a sample consisting of 1.100 children from Reykjavik and their mothers. The children were aged 5-15, all born between 1950 and 1960. The sample consisted of 100 subjects in each age group, equally divided between sexes. The interviews concerned data about family background, child rearing habits and other information about family ecology.

Results: Among other things: The construction of a scale of class, by means of classification of occupation, has been achieved. There is both a contradiction to and support of prevailing common sense theories and equalitarian patterns of culture. Regarding pervasiveness of class differences, both indicators from the material infrastructure of class, as well as from the psychosocial structure and the functioning of the personality, are part of the stratification dynamics. Three salient features accentuate the generalised patterns of social inequality. Underprivilege obtains, first and most generally, among women and girls and increases with the class position of their family. Second, it obtains for children of the lower classes, particularly the blue collar working class. Third, it obtains in the group of children from the entrepreneurial class. In summing up the three cases of special underprivilege, each seems to represent but a special case of the general patterns that appears and reappears in the data. They are but the most conspicuous elements of the pervasive structure of socio-educational, socialisatory and cognitive inequality, that characterises the social system as it is transformed from a predominantly rural culture, into a highly developed industrial society.

* * *

Dagvistarkönnun *i Vesterbæ: könnun gerð í Reykjavík í mars 1978 hjá börnum á aldrinum 0-10 ára*/A Study of Daycare in the West Area: An Investigation of 0-10 Year Old Children in Reykjavik During March 1978. Reykjavík: Ibúasamtök Vesturbæjar, 1979. In Icelandic.

Summary: In 1977, the Association of Inhabitants of the West area of Reykjavík decided to collaborate on children's daycare. As a consequence of this, information was collected about the parents' situation and their wishes. The study included all 0-10 year-old children in the area.

Theoretical frame of reference: Not explicitly expressed, but a sociologically oriented study on a statistical basis.

Method employed: A Questionnaire sent to the parents of 658 children in the area and to a sample consisting of the parents of every fourth child in the south area (258 children). 75% of the children in the west area and 70% in the south area answered.

Results: There was a need for increased daycare facilities. 50% attended the district schools. In the district school of Vesturbæjar, the number of square meters per child, was smaller than in all other schools in Reykjavík. The parents were worried about the traffic and there was a lack of space for outdoor activities, as well as for social activities. 78% of the parents wanted daycare arrangements for their children. Only 30% of the children were in daycare. There was a wish for flexible longer and more open-ing hours in the kindergartens. The parents wanted to participate more actively in the administration of the daycare centres.

* * *

Kristjánsdóttir, J. (1979). Könnun á aðstæðum félagsmanna/Survey of the Conditions of Members of the Association of Single Parents. In *Afmælisrit Félags einstæðra foreldra.* Reykavík, FEF, pp 17-18. In Icelandic.

Summary: A study of the situation of single parents, conducted in 1979 with a number of members of the Association of Single Parents. Several variables were studied, such as age, sex, marital status, housing conditions and occupation of those who joined the association in 1975-1978.

Theoretical frame of reference: A statistical and empirically based study.

Method employed: A mail questionnaire of 450 single parents (411 mothers and 39 fathers).

Results: All together the 411 mothers had 811 children. 56% were di-vorced, 36.9% were unmarried and 6% were widows. 42.3% lived in rented appartments, 29% owned their housing and 27.7% lived with relatives. The biggest occupational groups, consisted of clerks and unskilled manual workers. The groups of unemployed and housewives, could not be easily separated. The 39 fathers had 51 children. The proportion of divorced fathers was bigger than in an earlier study conducted in 1974-1975. The proportion of divorced fathers was 66.6%, widows 23%, and 10.2% were un-married. The biggest occupational group consisted of skilled workers.

* * *

Kristjánsdóttir, P. (1983). *Forskólareynsla og skólaganga: tengsl mis-munandi forskólareynslu við gangi og aðlögun í grunnskóla*/The Experience of Preschool Teaching and School Progres: Relations Between Different Influences of Preschool Upon Achievement and Social Adjustment in Elementary School. Reykjávík: IŠunn. In Icelandic.

Summary: A longitudinal study conducted in 1969-1979, of the influence of one year of preschool teaching at the age of six, upon subsequent school achievement, up to the final year of obligatory school, as well as upon the social development.

Theoretical frame of reference: An empirical study within the frames of educational psychology.

Method employed: Levin's school-maturity test was used on two groups of 6 year-olds in two preschools in Reykjávík. Some of the children received teaching and some did not. In 1970, all of the children were retested with Levin's test and a reading test. Every year, the children were tested on various school subjects, as well as on their social development.

Results: After 9 years in school, no differences in school achievement were found between the children who had received preschool teaching and those who had not.

* * *

Magnússon, M.V. & T. Valsson (1977). *Könnun á viŠhorfum mæŠra til barnauppeldis*/A Study of Mothers' Views on Child rearing. Reykjávík: Háskóli Islands, Félagsvísindadeild. In Icelandic.

Summary: A study of mothers' rearing attitudes, regarding discipline, liberality and protection. Their attitudes towards sex-roles, sexuality, school, media influence, etc., are also studied.

Theoretical frame of reference: An empirical study within the frames of educational and developmental psychology.

Method employed: A Likert-scale Questionnaire, of a random sample of 203 mothers (116 from Reykjávík and 87 from Húsavík) with children born in 1961, 1967 and 1971. Conclusions based upon significance and correlation computations. The reliability of questions correlations was tried out according to Spearman's test of inner stability.

Results: The most significant differences were found regarding age, education and occupation. Mothers born before 1940, with poor education and married to skilled, or unskilled workers, were more disciplinary and protective than others, as well as more traditional in their views on sex-roles and sexuality.

* * *

Oláfsdóttir, E. R., S. Jökulsdóttir & V. Jánusdóttir (1985). *Forsendur lestrarnáms*/Preconditions of Learning How to Read. Reykjavik: Kennaraháskoli Islands. In Icelandic.

Summary: A study of eight 6-7 year-old children, of whom five were able to read, while three were beginners. The aim of the study was to ascertain how children learn to read.

Theoretical frame of reference: Based upon a review of existing literature, which has been related to an empirically based investigation.

Method employed: A linguistic study, based on reading tests.

* * *

Traustadóttir, S. (1984). *Om at være enslig mor på Island: et glimt inn i et kulturlandskap*/To Be a Single Mother on Iceland: A View of a Cultural Landscape. Trondheim: Institutt for Sosiologi og Samfunnskunnskap. In Norwegian.

Summary: A study of single mothers in Reykjavík, of their living conditions, their experience of their situation, as well as of the attitudes of society. The main question is: What is it in society that makes it different to live as a single mother?

Theoretical frame of reference: A sociological study, aiming to understand and explain the author's differentiated experiences in Iceland and Norway, respectively. Within the frames of Tönnies theory: Gesellschaft - Gemeinschaft (Man in society, society in man).

Method employed: Structured interviews with both qualitative and quantitative data used for official information.

* * *

NORWEGIAN BIBLIOGRAPHY

YOUNG CHILDREN'S MATERIAL CONDITIONS

Hansen, A. & A. S. Andersen (1984). *Barns levekår*/Children's Standard of Living. Oslo: Statistisk Sentralbyrå, Statistiske Analyser 53. ISBN 82-537-2065-3. ISSN 0333-0621. In Norwegian. Part of the publication is translated into English.

Summary: A description and analysis of important aspects of children's standard of living.

Theoretical frame of reference: Not explicitly expressed, but a sociological approach with importance attached to empirical data.

Method employed: Based on "Survey of Standard of Living 1973", "Health Survey 1975", "Survey of Transport and Welfare 1979", "Survey of Standard of Living 1980" and the "Time Budget Survey 1980-81".

Results: Changes in children's living conditions in this century: Here, the focus is placed on the relations among some of these conditions, such as serious antagonism in the home, parents' illness, poor economy and difficulties in providing food. The profile of the standard of living has changed. Until the 1930ies, about 60% of the population was exposed to one or more of these problems. Since then, the proportion declined strongly to 40% in the 1950ies and 1960ies. That more and more people are spared exposure to these problems, is partly due to the fact that the total number of problems has declined and partly to the fact that the existing problems, to a higher degree, are concentrated on the same individuals. Children and their families: Before world war one, every third person was younger than 16 years old. In the beginning of the 1980s the figure was less than every fourth. 89% were living in families with married parents. Less than 11% were living in single parent families. More than 90% were living in households with only one family. Every fourth child was an only child. Children's social background: Nearly all of the children have fathers who are working. 36% are unskilled workers, 41.9% are salaried employees, 8.2% are farmers or fishermen and 13.4% have other self-employed work. Half of the mothers are working. 6.9% are unskilled workers, 36.6% are salaried employees, 4.3% are farmers or fishermen and 49.1 work at home. In single parent's families, 26% are unskilled workers, 48% salaried employees and 26% work at home. 24% of the fathers left school after primary school, 25.8% after secondary school level I, 24.5% after secondary school level II and 25.7% had an university education. Of the mothers 25% had primary school, 48% secondary school level I, 11.3% secondary school level II and 15.7% had an university education. Parents' work: Both parents working full-time; 14%, one or both of the parents working part-time; 43% and one of the parents unemployed 43%. Of the single parents, 68% worked full-time and 32% worked part-time. Childcare arrangements: About 40% of the children cared for by others than the parents, are minded by relatives or friends. More than 20% are cared for by childminders, maids and so on. 44% of the children are cared for in daycare centres. Time spent with parents: As an average, mothers and children spent 6.6 hours together every day and fathers and children 4.1 hours. Single parents spent 5.8 and 4.2 hours, respectively. The whole household spent, as an average, 2.7 hours together in families of cohabiting parents, and 3.4 hours in single parent families. Contact with adult relatives: 2/3 of the children with cohabiting parents, have contact with their parents at least once a week, while the figure was 41% in single parent families. 13% and 36%, respectively had contact less than once a month. 52% and 35%, respectively, had contact with other adult relatives at least once a week. The figures for contact less than once a month was 22% and 38%, respectively.

* * *

Holter, H. (1975). *Familien i klassesamfunnet/*The Family in Class Society. Oslo: Pax. ISBN 82-530-06-52-7. In Norwegian.

Summary: The following questions are highlighted: Are we moving towards a stunted family form? What is the relationship between oppression of women and oppression of the classes? Does society want obedient working class children? The family is viewed in relation to official family policy, to historical development and to the attitudes that children are brought up to in different social classes are highlighted. Finally, it is discussed, how the method of studying individual families can tell us something about society in general.

Theoretical frame of reference: Within a sociological and social-psychological frame.

Method employed: Detached historical and theoretical analysis of psychological data from the "Family Research" carried out by The Institute of Society Research and The Institute of Psychology, The University of Oslo in 1969.

Results: I: The elaboration of family-political aims and means, are partly dependent on the distinction between the public and private fields of authorities. Clarified with examples from eastern Europe and China and a short outline of Norwegian family policy from 1930 and 1970. The family policy is characterised by a missing connection between the practical policy and more principal views of the family and of a missing recognition of the contradictions between the family policy and society in other respects. II: The tendencies in the intimate family relations can be said to be individualising, privatising, intimidating and mystifying, to differing degrees in the working class and the middle class. III: The class distinctions of the family forms are discussed. IV: Attitudes towards sex roles are general across the class barriers but also have a specific form in each class. V: The socialisation values of the working class have to be understood in the light of both the position of the class as suppressed and its forms of resistance against the suppression. VI: The network of the working class family in becoming less and less family orientated. This is not only the result of economic and housing conditions, but is also a social-psychological entrenchment against middle class cultural elements, meant as a defence of class interest. The middle class network has a more offensive character and expresses, among other things, the economic and ideological hegemony of the class. VII: The first part of the family research, was characterised by a quantitative recording of the isolated, external phenomena of the family, while the last part represents a con-

phenomena of the family, while the last part represents a concentration of a qualitative description of the internal contradictions in the individual family. To avoid confusion and absorption in the individual family, it was necessary to pick out "typical" families.

* * *

Lingsom, S. & A. L. Ellingsæter (1983). *Arbeid, fritid og samvær. Erindringer i tidsbruk i 70-årene*/Work, Leisure and Being Together. Changes in Time Use in the 1970s. Oslo: Statistisk Sentralbyrå. Statistiske Analyser, 49. ISBN 82-537-1924-8. In Norwegian and English.

Summary: A comprehensive analysis of how different groups in the population spend their time, and of how time-use has changed in the 1970s.

Theoretical frame of reference: Not explicitly expressed, but within a sociological theoretical frame. A strongly empirically directed survey.

Method employed: A national random sample of a total of 5049 persons of 17-74 years of age, by means of diaries. Statistically preparated.

Results: Time-use patterns have changed considerably for both men and women since the beginning of the 1970s. The changes are most pronounced for women, where there has been a reduction in the time spent on housework, which is now used primarily on leisure activities and on paid work. Families with only one breadwinner, decreased from 50% in 1971-72, to 28% in 1980-81. Only men in families with young children, have responded to women's new employment situation, by spending more time on household work and family care. The only employment combination which gives an equal work load for both sexes, is where the husband is employed full-time and the woman part-time. The difference between men's and women's work load, however, has been reduced in the 1970s. There has been a general increase in leisure time, and the activities which have increased most are

mostly spend their leisure time outside the home, with friends, etc. In general, time spent with non-family was extensive for young persons and decreased with age for both men and women. Time spent with the children is influenced less by the parents' employment situation, than commonly assumed, but is strongly influenced by the age of the children.

* * *

Strømsheim, G. (1983). Den sårbara likestilling. Arbeidstidsmønstre, familieroller og institusjonell avhengighet i tre typer barnefamilier/The Vulnerable Equality. Patterns of Working Time, Family Roles and Institutional Dependence in Three Types of Families With Children. In C. Wadel et al., *Dagliglivets organisering*/The Organisation of Everyday Life. Oslo: Universitetsforlaget. ISBN 82-00-06611-8. In Norwegian.

Summary: A demonstration of connections between working hours, the segmentation of the labour market and equality between the sexes. An illustration of how the families organise, of the consequences for their connection with the labour market and for the relationship between the spouses.

Theoretical frame of reference: Social-anthropological approach based on feministic theories.

Method employed: Case studies of 3 "constructed" family-types.

Results: The conditions of the families are different, but the parents have to adjust to interests and wants and often disagree upon economic security, equality, family solidarity and self realisation. Both men and women experience new demands regarding the traditional sex roles. In society, the conditions of equality regarding work- and family roles are badly adjusted. The sex differences in work- and family life are still very distinct, but at the same time, new patterns offer possibilities for a greater freedom for women and men, with regard the to different spectra of roles, that both sexes can obtain in society.

* * *

Leira, A. (1983). Kvinners organisering av dagliglivet: Hverdagspraksis i et eldre bystrøk/Women's Organisation of Everyday Life. Everyday Routine in an Old Urban Quarter. In C. Wadel et al., *Dagliglivets organisering*/The Organisation of Everyday Life. Oslo: Universitetsforlaget. ISBN 82-00-06611-8. In Norwegian.

Summary: A description of the complexity of and the variations in women's employment, of the main kinds of women's work and of how the different kinds are combined in individual employment patterns, of how women's different work patterns are mutually connected and of how they create assumptions of their own and of others' work situation. Central assumptions for the employment strategies described, are discussed: The improvement of a local part-time labour market for women, sex roles and the division of housework, and a neighbourhood culture, developed and maintained by younger women.

Theoretical frame of reference: A sociological approach based on feministic theories.

Method employed: Observations of and interviews with 15 25-45 year-old women with children living at home, most of them young children, in an old, central part of Oslo in the late 1970s about work- and cooperation forms.

Results: The organisation of everyday life in this part of the city shows, that women's work cannot only be described as regular paid work and as household obligations. Other institutional frames, such as relationships, friendships and neighbourships, must also be considered in this connection. In addition to regularly paid and unpaid work, there are different kinds of "grey" and "black" work, which can be arranged through close social relations, or the social network, or through informal help arrangements.

* * *

YOUNG CHILDREN'S SOCIAL CONDITIONS

Andenæs, A. Gode rutiner og gode følelser. Dagligliv og utvikling i småbarnsfamilien/Good Routines and Good Feelings. Everyday Life and Development in the Family With Young Children. I *Tidsskrift for Nordisk forening for pedagogisk forskning 5, 3.* In Norwegian. With an English summary.

Summary: Tells about everyday life in Norwegian families with young children. With the main focus on sorting out the pattern of details constituting everyday life. This pattern is perceived as a key to understand children's socialiation and development.

Theoretical frame of reference: Within the framework of critical psychology.

Method employed: Based on existing research of the conditions and content of family life, especially in the Nordic countries.

Results: Social conditions of special importance to the organisation and content of family life, such as gender-specificity of parenthood and the family's isolation from the rest of the society, are pointed out. These constitute the frames of interaction in the family, and have to be integrated in analysis made in family research. Furthermore, a description of the performance of life-form interview is given, with two main examples.

* * *

Andenæs, A. & T. Andreassen (1980). *Drabantbyfamilien som oppvekstmiljø for fireåringer. Utprøvning af en teoretisk og empirisk tilnærmning til studiet av sosialisering*/The Suburban Family As a Rearing Environment for 4 year-olds. A Test of a Theoretical and Empirical Approach to the Study of Socialisation. Oslo: Universitetet, Psykologisk Institut. Hovedopgave. ISBN 82-569-0485-2. In Norwegian.

Socialization of Young Children in the Nordic Countries

Summary: A contribution to the theoretical basis of the analysis of family socialization and of correlation in ordinary families, which brings the 4 year-old child into focus. With a basis in general social conditions, the care functions in the families are analysed, in order to explain how they determine the correlation in the family.

Theoretical frame of reference: A theoretical interdisciplinary approach based on a context model, showing that conditions at one level determine the elaboration of phenomena at the level underneath.

Method employed: Qualitative interviews with 12 mothers of 4 year-olds - half of them girls and the other half boys, representing ordinary suburban families.

Results: Among other things: That the child's meeting with the sex segregated society is very simplified, that the mother is responsible for affairs in the home and for the well-being of everyone in the family, while the father leaves in the morning and returns at dinnertime. This limits, to a considerable degree, the possibilities of the surburban family for gaining experience of the society of which it is part and of which the child will be a member later on. The tendency of personifying what happens in the family, reduces the child's chances to learn to collaborate in joint cases of importance for others. Some of the families, though, make more of the possibilities than others. The parents' structuring of the play situation and their control of the behaviour and day and night rythm, make it possible for the child to learn to organise and control its own behaviour. It is through entering into relationships with other people, that the child acquires skills and qualities, which we connect with being a human being. These relations are rooted in and can be understood from the perspective of the society that the children and parents are living in. The use of games, humor, ambiguities and exaggerated reactions in the families, represent strategies on the parents' side which bring about the performance of desired behaviour. But in a way, that gives the child the possibility to attribute the initiative to itself.

* * *

Berentzen, S. (1979). Et samhandlingsperspektiv på studiet av barn/An Interaction Perspective in the Study of Children. In *Tidsskrift for samfunnsforskning, 20, 393-415.* In Norwegian. With an English summary.

Summary: The study takes up certain aspects of a methodical change in the study of children, where the significance of exploring the children's competence for social participation and the content of their interaction, is focused. The interaction-perspective is illustrated with the study of the social organisation in a Norwegian kindergarten and a study of the street life in a black ghetto in USA. The intention here, is to show how sex identity can function as a fundamental "resource", when the child defines social situations and develops interaction systems.

Theoretical frame of reference: Within an interactional frame, with importance attached to the empirical illumination of natural interaction.

Method employed: The kindergarten: Daily observations of 10 boys and 11 girls aged of 5-7 years for 6 months in a Norwegian kindergarten. Observations of boys and girls aged of 8-18 years in a black ghetto in Philadelphia.

Results: The child participates in the development of organised interaction within different settings. The importance of analysing how different settings form interaction conditions, and how social competence and concepts are "transferred" between different settings, is stressed.

* * *

Berentzen, S. (1980). *Kjønnskontrasten i barns lek. Analyse av forholdet mellom begrebsdannelse og samhandling i en barnehage*/Gender Specific Contrasts in Children's Play. Analysis of the Relationship Between the Formation of Concepts and Interaction in a

Kindergarten. Bergen: Universitetet i Bergen. Sosialantropologisk Institut, 1980. Skriftserie, no. 3. In Norwegian.

Summary: Observations in a kindergarten, with a view to analysis of both cultural and organisational aspects of the spontaneous interaction between children.

Theoretical frame of reference: Within a social-anthropological frame.

Method employed: Systematic participant observations of 5-6 year-olds in a kindergarten.

Results: The criterion of boys and girls concerning estimation of behaviour, was different. They showed contempt for each others' achievements. The boys estimate each others' achievements according to strength, speed and courage, while the important thing for the girls was "to be in the game", to mark the alliance with another girl and to change partners. In these alliances, the girls "fight" to be the "mother". Through this identification and by making the other girls accept this, they achieved the highest possible position. The boys' play can be seen as a social system which easily provokes situations, that are spoiling the games, while the girls know to a higher degree what to play and how to play it. The boys' games are more varied than the girls'. They are "object" or "material" orientated, while the girls' games are not. The analysed cultural processes of the interaction of children within a given "setting", shows the general "mechanisms" behind the cognitive development taking place spontaneously. Furthermore, it is shown how sex identity acts as the fundamental structure, where experience is encoded and systematised.

* * *

Bækholt, S. (1981). *Venter på far. En analyse av åtte arbeiderklassefedres forhold til barn og familieliv*/Waiting for Daddy. An Analysis of Eight Working class Fathers' Relationships to Child and Family Life. Oslo: Universitetet i Oslo, Psykologisk Institut, arbeidsrapport, 6. ISBN 82-569-0540-9.

Summary: A survey, firstly, of the interaction between fathers and their children and an evaluation of the developmental possibilities of this interaction, and secondly, of the correlations between the father-child interaction and the social and material conditions of the family.

Theoretical frame of reference: A qualitative description and analysis of the actual interaction in the family.

Method employed: Detailed life-style interviews with 8 fathers of 3-6 year old children. Skilled industrial workers with honorary offices on different levels and working in factories in the same branch.

Results: The way that the fathers are attached to working life reduces their possibilities to contribute to the development of the child. It is not only a question of time, but of the way that time is organised. The fathers seem to be more active and reflective in situations, where they are left alone with the child. The analysis of the distribution of responsibilities and tasks in the families, shows a clearly gender-related pattern, where the father participates more in order to do the mother a favour, than because of the necessity of the task. Besides materially based hindrances, the emotional sides of the relationship between the parents causes hindrances for equal participation.

* * *

Gullestad, M. (1984). *Kitchen-table Society. A Case Study of the Family Life and Friendships of Young Working Class Mothers in Urban Norway*. Oslo: Universitetsforlaget, ISBN 82-00-06778-5. In English.

Summary: Survey of working class mothers with young children in Bergen, the second largest town in Norway, of their mutual contacts and especially of how they organise their family lives, their social networks and of how they reflect on this.

Theoretical frame of reference: Feministic, social-anthropological study.

Method employed: A longitudinal study of a girlfriend network. Qualitative methods of participant observation with statistical indicies of examined problems.

Results: Who fits in with whom? Shaped by factors, such as occupation, region, religion and urban versus rural background. They define themselves as respectable, ordinary people with a nice home. Hearth and home: They have become more strongly integrated in the market economy. This is one of the reasons that they are able to enter into roles and activities outside "hearth and home". Motherhood and marriage: Motherhood is a fundamental identity, as both role and motherhood have a great influence on, what young mothers do. This is also demonstrated in cases of marriage crisis and divorce. The mother is the central figure in the home, and the father is the one who is "thrown out", or who has to leave. Acquiring a home: Once they are allotted, appartments seldom revert to the letting agency again. Many young families want to live close to where they grew up and to their parents, and the parents also make participation in activities outside home possible. Visiting and other social occasions in the home: Informal visiting and more formalised occasions in the homes, set the stage for much sociability between friends and relatives. This is a sign of the home-centredness of Norwegian culture. Public fora, where one can meet friends and relatives are few, due to the home-centredness and the expense, late urbanisation and pietist religious attitudes. Paid work: Most women work part-time, a few work full-time, and a few have no, or little paid work. The kind of work, that they have, is often ambiguous as a field for self-realisation and a sign of identity. The differences between the sexes, in terms of class position and wages, are relatively small compared to other groups. Going out: Combining family life and going out to discotheques, e.g. accentuates conflicts between individuality and hearth and home, by also providing moral dilemmas. Womens' moral discourse and its consequences for female solidarity and conflict: The moral discourse is very concrete and personal. Control is a key concept, which is related to identities as "decent ordinary people". Married life: A wife is always responsible for the administration of some of the money, even if the overview and control lie with the husband. Division of work between the spouses is obiviously changing, even if the change is more ideological than practical. But it is a new way of codifying the unity of the household. Reflections on being a woman: Women are strong, enterprising and culture-building. They play a crucial role in creating and maintaining family networks and family life-style.

* * *

Haavind, H. (1979). Analyse av socialisering i småbarnsfamilier/Analysis of Socialisation in Families with Young Children. In *Tidsskrift for samfunnsforskning, 20, 447-472*. In Norwegian.

Summary: A study of socialisation in families with young children. The aim is to describe in what ways the life of the families is embedded in certain objective social conditions, which are subjectively transformed by individuals to create their personal world.

Theoretical frame of reference: A sociological approach with a psychological point of departure.

Method employed: An empirical study of families from urban areas, with at least one child of 4 years of age. Group talks and personal interviews with the mothers.

Results: Some cultural frames for interpretation of events within the families are presented. The aim is to make them explicit and to show, how actual interpretations differ according to frames. The frames suitable for psychological analysis must be related to objective social conditions. Four such cultural frames are discussed. Common features, as well as variations between the families in interaction, are analysed. A model for coordination of the different kinds of considerations, which may govern the mothers' behaviour towards the child in actual situations, is presented. Examples of characteristics of some mothers are given and discussed. The analysis is completed by pointing to some developmental consequences for the child.

* * *

Haavind, H. (1984). Fordeling af omsorgsfunksjoner i småbarnsfamilier/The Distribution of the Caring Functions in Families With Young Children. In I. Rudie (red.), *Myk start - hard landing.* Oslo: Universitetsforlaget. ISBN 82-00-07057-3. In Norwegian.

Summary: A study of how the tasks in the home are distributed between the husband and the wife, when they have young children, of how the distribution develops as a result of the interaction between the spouses, through the way they behave towards each other and to the surroundings.

Theoretical frame of reference: Not explicitly expressed.

Method employed: Individual interviews with the mothers in about 100 families, all living in a larger city with one 4 year-old child and belonging to different social classes. Also control interviews with some of the fathers, both individually and in groups.

Results: Changes in the family are not only dependent on changes in the social conditions outside the family. The main emphasis is placed on the organisation of time, but lack of time is an explanation that must not be overemphasised in relation to the distribution of the caring functions. The mother is responsible for creating routines, for adjusting life to new circumstances, and for the administration of the tasks. The father can participate in single tasks, if he wants to and if he has the time. He intimates that he has a good relationship to his children and it is enough for him to show this now and again. He gives his children a lot, but it is the mother who has the reponsibility of taking care of them.

* * *

Haug, P. (1982). *Foreldre, barn og barnehage, samarbeid om oppse-ding*/Parents, Children and Kindergarten, Cooperation in Rearing. Oslo: Det norske samlaget. ISBN 82-521-2151-9. In Norwegian.

Summary: The relations between the parents and the kindergarten. The pattern and the tendencies of the Norwegian kindergarten organisation, are illuminated.

Theoretical frame of reference: A human ecological/pedagogical approach.

Method employed: The results are based on differnt quantitatively treated statistical data and on a questionnaire completed by 25 pedagogues from different kindergartens, about the relations among themselves and with the 472 children.

Results: The cooperation between the parents and the institution is concentrated around exchange of information and less around discussions of goals and content. The kindergarten tradition is concerned with the contact to the parents, but it is the parents who are the offensive and dominating parties in this contact, although there is a tendency that this is changing. Because of the very stringent framework of the kindergarten and the daily workload, decentralisation is restrained. The expediency of the existing forms of cooperation is brought into question. The contact that takes place, in the form of the parents' bringing and collecting the children, is not sufficient. The process of promoting the contact, is a question of larger appropriations, and is therefore a question of willingness on the part of the executives.

* * *

Kalleberg, A. (1983). Foreldreskift og kjønnsrolleforandring/Parental Shift and Sex-role Changes. In C. Wadel et al., *Dagliglivets organisering*/Organisation of Everyday Life. Oslo: Universitetsforlaget. ISBN 82-00-06611-8. In Norwegian.

Summary: When the parents work different hours, so that one is at home minding the child, it is called parental shift. The parental tasks are of primary importance, but taking turns at it, the parents have little opportunity of being with the children at the same time. This can be seen as a special form of equality between women and men. The problem is illustrated by 3 case studies.

Theoretical frame of reference: Not explicitly expressed, but within a sociological frame.

Method employed: Based on material from interviews with about 130 two-parent families with young children, from different cities and places in Norway, in the period 1975-1978.

Results: Parental shifts appear as a peculiar family organisational practice, which makes it difficult for both husband and wife to maintain the traditional sex roles. But the shifts do not remove all barriers against equality. The practice of a conscious ideology of equality, seems to foresee more radical institutional changes. Families trying out their concepts of equality through parental shifts, acquire experiences that they did not have a complete overview of previously. Sociologically, this lends coherence to the view, that equality, as well as traditional sex role attitudes, must considerably be modified through practice.

* * *

Kalleberg, A. (1985). *165 Oslo-familier: Forsørgerstrategier, dagligliv og likestilling*/165 Families From Oslo: Breadwinner Strategies, Everyday life and Equality. Oslo: Institut for samfunnsforskning.

Summary: An overview of the research design and preliminary results of a family study in 1983. Among other things, a survey of working hours/labour market connection, childcare and division of household tasks in 165 two-income families with minor children, is given. How the organisation of the spouses' working hours influences their leisure time and the patterns of being together in the family, whether there is accordance between the attitudes of the spouses concerning equality, and of how these are acted upon.

Theoretical frame of reference: A strongly empirically directed sociological approach.

Method employed: Based on interviews with a random dimensional sample of 165 two-income families with minor children, living in Oslo. Including 165 families with at least one child younger than 10 years. All together, the families have 315 children living at home. Both spouses were interviewed and special sampling procedures were used, in order to allow for comparisons between families in different social classes and between women in selected occupational groups.

Results: The main difference in provider strategies are related to class. However, relative resource differences between husband and wife, measured by their educational level, occupational status and income, also seem to be important factors in determining family working hour patterns, division of household tasks and childcare arrangements.

* * *

Kvalheim, J. L. (1980). *Barns læring af sociale roller*/Children's Learning of Social Roles. Oslo: Universitetsforlaget. ISBN 82-00-27492-6. In Norwegian.

Summary: A survey from a kindergarten, of childrens' play and of the organisation of their joint play, with a view to observing the learning process connected with order-creating, in childrens' understanding of social play. Concerning what children have in common in their understanding, how they learn it and the transfer of cultural patterns from one generation to the next.

Theoretical frame of reference: Not explicitly expressed, but a social-antropological approach with the involvement of pedagogical and psychological aspects.

Method employed: Both passive and active observations of children being active together and with adults. Also, quantitative interviews with 15 of the 18 parents. Partly in their homes and partly in the kindergarten.

Results: The learning process, which is part of the socialisation of the child, is defined as the transfer of behaviour from adults to children, in the child's social environment. The child will try the behaviour out in play and in other connections. Through feedback from the other participants in the situation, the child will gradually learn the behaviour, which from the child's point of view gives the best opportunities for admittance and acceptance in the group. The kindergarten as a place of work, is problematic, especially with regard to management and the division of work. The kindergarten must be structured such, that the children's needs for group belonging are considered. For example, by establishing age differentiated "brother- and sister groups". The adults must see to it that the children receive the opportunity for spontaneously organised play. The groups must not be to big, or be spread over the whole house, since this could lead to the children not knowing where they belong.

* * *

Nafstad, H. E. & S. Gaarder (1979). *Barn - utvikling og miljø. Om samspillet mellom hjem. barnhage og (lokal) samfund*/Children - Development and Environment. About the Correlation between Home, Kindergarten and (the Local) Community. Oslo: Tiden norsk forlag. ISBN 82-10-01745-4. In Norwegian.

Summary: Survey of the living conditions of children in Norway. Status of knowledge, theory and methods, that are necessary in preventive work and in the work concerning the children's well-being and development in a broader sense. Development of methods and types of surveys to illustrate connections in the conditions of growth and cognitve and emotional development of groups of 3-7 year-old children.

Theoretical frame of reference: Not explicitly expressed, but within an interdisciplinary sociological frame.

Method employed: Theoretical analysis based on existing research within a broad frame.

Results: The child is looked upon as a social being. Experiences and actions are described within a social frame of reference. The developmental theory evolved, has its point of origin in the interaction of emotional, cognitive and social aspects. Up-to-date knowledge of the development of young children and their growth conditions.

* * *

Nafstad, H. E. (1976). *Barnehagen som oppvekstmiljø og arbeidsplass*/The Kindergarten as a Rearing Environment and as a Place of Work. Oslo, Tiden Norsk Forlag: ISBN 82-10-01307-6. In Norwegian. With an English summary.

Summary: A reprint of 2 reports: "Hva slags daginstitusjon trenger barn?" A survey of Norwegian Kindergarten personnels' estimation of the kindergartens in 1974. "De voksne i barnehagen" from 1975, is about the functions of the personnel and has as its objective to support the planners and administrators in analysing the strengths and consequences of different kindergarten systems.

Theoretical frame of reference: Not explicitly expressed. An approach to show connections between the macro- , micro- and individual level.

Method employed: Quantitative survey based on interviews with kindergarten personnel. 1438 persons (60% of all personnel) from 367 kindergartens (88,5% of all kindergartens) in Norway in 1972.

Results: 1: A presentation of the method used, a discussion of how long the child ought to be in kindergarten every day, of the relationship between school and kindergarten, of how the kindergarten can replace possibilities that no longer exist in today's society and finally, of how the kindergarten can undertake tasks of both primary and secondary character. 2: A review of the educational background of the personnel, and evaluation of important aspects in their working situation and of their future work plans.

* * *

Smith, L. (1983). Foreldres omsorgsfunksjon og småbarns omsorgs-behov/Childcare and the Affiliative Needs of Young Children. In *Tidsskrift for norsk psykologforening, 20, 119-127.* With an English summary.

Summary: An examination of the concepts of maternal deprivation and mother-infant attachment, with some applied illustrations.

Theoretical frame of reference: Not explicitly expressed, but an approach within developmental psychology and child psychiatry.

Method employed: Review of recent studies challenging the view, that the first years of life necessarily have crucial effects upon later development.

Results: It is concluded, that deleterious influences must continue for a long time, in order to be of much importance. The malleability of early human development is documented by examining the prognoses of children, who were brought up in adverse environments and who were subsequently adopted.

* * *

YOUNG CHILDREN'S CULTURAL CONDITIONS

Bergem, T. & S. Sandsmark (1980). *Slik foreldrene ser det. En undersøkelse blant foreldre med barn i menighets- og organisasjonsbarnehager i Hordaland*/As the Parents See It. A Survey Among Parents in Church- and Organisation Kindergartens in Hordaland. Bergen, Norsk Lærerakademi. Skriftserie. In Norwegian.

Summary: Results of a questionnaire completed by parents with children in church- and organisation kindergartens, about the christian object's clause formulated for a great number of Norwegian kindergartens.

Theoretical frame of reference: Not explicitly expressed, but a sociological approach, directed by importance attached to the empirical side.

Method employed: A questionnaire completed by the parents of children in 32 kindergartens, 78% of them public and 19% private. The preparation is statistical.

Results: An overwhelming majority of the Norwegian people want their child to be reared in a christian way (46% for, 21% not sure and 33% against). 86% of the parents think that the christian values are stressed as much as they want them to be. 10% think that they are stressed too much, and 4% want it to be stressed more strongly.

* * *

Evenshaug, O. (1981). *Barnedåp og oppdragelse: hva ønsker og mener småbarnsforeldre i storbyen?*/Baptism and Rearing: What Do Parents of Young Children in the City Wish and Think. Oslo: Luther Forlag A/S. ISBN 82-531-7357-1. In Norwegian.

Summary: The wishes and opinions of parents concerning the christian education of their children in the home, the church and in society. An illustration of the relationship between baptism and the rearing intentions of the parents, seen in connection with their social and cultural background, and of a few other sides of the child's rearing environment.

Theoretical frame of reference: Psychological and sociological research and formation of theories concerning the role and importance of the family in the process of socialisation.

Method employed: Intensive, both qualitatively and quantitatively treated interviews with 257 mothers of 4 year-olds in their homes in Oslo. Hermeneutical analysis.

Results: Does baptism have any relation to rearing intentions: 69% answered yes, 9% little, 11% none at all. 9% did not know and 3% did not answer. There are 3 different attitudes towards christian intentions in rearing. Intentions based on belief: Christian rearing is not only based on pedagogical, phychological and/or ethical principles, but first and foremost on the belief of the truth and worth of christianity in itself. Intentions based on tradition: It is not so much the worth of christianity in itself, as the pedagogical, mental hygienic and ethical aspects, as well as the wish to carry on a tradition, that characterise this opinion. Intentions based on acceptance of reality: More reserved towards christian rearing and christian influence, both in kindergarten and school.

* * *

Evenshaug, O. & D. Hallen (1983). *Hvem skal oppdra barna? Pedagogisk ansvarsfordeling i hjem og samfunn*/Who Is Going to Rear the Children. The Distribution of Pedagogical Responsibility in the Home and in Society. Oslo: Gyldendal norsk forlag. ISBN 82-05-15100-8. In Norwegian.

Summary: The question of distribution of the pedagogical responsibility in and outside the home and between the parents, is illustrated. Made topical in connection with the increased participation of women in the labour market.

Theoretical frame of reference: Not explicitly expressed, but a theoretical, as well as a sociological approach, with importance attached to the empirical side.

Method employed: Analysis of interviews from 1975-76, with 257 mothers of young children in Oslo. Part of the SOFU-project. Qualitative preparation.

Results: Consequences for the family and society: The mothers see, in an unreflected way, the responsibility as being parental. Family- and child policies do not contribute to the weakening of custody and parental consciousness of pedagogical responsibility. In principle, the parental responsibility is to be shared, but many mothers experience the actual distribution to be oblique concerning the home and the pedagogical institutions, as well as between the parents. As to the obliquity between the home and the institutions, this varies depending on whether the mother is working full-time, or part-time. In the first case, the mother thinks that too much responsibility is placed on the institution. There seems to be a conflict between the rate of work outside the home and wish to be responsible for rearing the child. Mothers working part time, look upon the institutions and other pedagogical offers, as a kind of relief and help, just as it can be too one-sided for the child to be at home all day. There is an indicated need of 10-30 hours per week for pedagogical offers of all kinds. Other pedagogical offers (music, sport, religion) are used by resourceful families, who are actually the ones who need it the least. Many mothers experience themselves as pedagogical single-parents. The mother feels guilty about not being able to fulfil the pedagogical role. The "dream" of most mothers with young children, is a part-time job - for both parents -The priority of child rearing and pedagogical activities, is low in society. However, it is up to society to create better conditions for the parents on the basis of local conditions, as well as working life, housing conditions and neighbourhood environment.

* * *

Fougner, J., Ø. Ramvi & F. Søbstad (1980). *Barn foran skjer-men*/Children in Front of the Screen. Oslo: Aschehoug, 1980. ISBN 82-03-12192-6. In Norwegian.

Summary: A discussion of questions concerning young children and television.

Theoretical frame of reference: Not explicitly expressed, but within a sociological frame with importance attached to the empirical side.

Method employed: Based on interviews with 264 preschool children (46% girls and 54% boys between 3 and 7 years old) and 49 nursery teachers, as well as on questionnaires of the children's parents. Carried through in 1977-79 in 20 kindergartens in Trondheim.

Results: Family situation: Group 1, consisting of families where one or both the parents had an academic education or a high working position (29%). Group 2, consisting of the social middle class (64%). Group 3, consisting of families where neither of the parents had any education beyond primary school. Television habits: Only 3 families had no television. 84% watched the children's programmes every day, or nearly every day. Of the parents, 41% watched television every day, and 46% several times a week. In group 1, 30% watched every day, in group 2, the figure was 43% and in group 3, 65%. 48% of the mothers watched the programmes together with the children every time, 92% several times a week. 26% of the fathers saw all of the children's programmes and 75% watched several times a week. 7% regularly watched programmes for adults, 26% once a week, 45% rarely, and 22% never. 39% of the children never dreamt about what they had seen, 47% sometimes did, while 14% often did. 53% of the children experienced fear, 13% got excited and 2,5% had nightmares. Many of the children identify themselves with what they see on television. 48% never play what they have seen on television, 23% play both at home and in the kindergarten, 26% only at home and 3% only in the kindergarten. 60% of the parents also usually read to the children. Concerning the analyses of the content of the different programmes reference must be made to the book.

* * *

Hodne, B. & S. Sogner, red. (1984). *Barn av sin tid. Fra norske barns historie*/Children of Their Time. From the History of Norwegian Children. Oslo: Universitetsforlaget, 1984. ISBN 82-00-07101-4. In Norwegian.

Summary: A description of the cultural history of Norwegian children during the last 200 years. Consisting of 14 articles about rearing and family - work, school, leisure - family and society and children and culture.

Theoretical frame of reference: Not explicitly expressed, but within a sociological frame.

Method employed: Based on written material about folk traditions and on elderly peoples' written memories of their childhood.

* * *

Tønnessen, L. K. (1982). *Slik levde småbarna før. Trek av barndommens historie i vårt land - med særlig vekt på de minste barnas liv og lek*/Children Lived Like This Then, Traits of the History of Young children in Our Country With Special Attention Drawn to the Life and Play of Young children. Oslo: Universitetsforlaget. ISBN 82-00-28630-4. In Norwegian.

Summary: A study of the history of 0-7 year old children, with special attention drawn to birth and care of young children, everyday life and rearing attitudes, festivals, illness and death and differences of conditions of life in different families.

Theoretical frame of reference: Not explicitly expressed.

Method employed: Based on material from bigger European historical works, especially Swedish. Concerning the Norwegian material no systematic reading of the source material has been made.

SWEDISH BIBLIOGRAPHY

YOUNG CHILDREN'S MATERIAL CONDITIONS

Barnfamiljernas *ekonomi*/The Economy of Families With Children (1975). SOU 1973:35. Stockholm: Socialdepartementet. Rapport nr. 5 från Barnmiljöutredningen. ISBN 91-38-02253-2. In Swedish.

Summary: A demonstration of differences between families with children and families without children, as well as differences among families with children. What are the differences in standard of economy? How are the economic resources that the families have at their disposal distributed among the families with children? How manifestations of family policy, social policy and tax policy change the relations among the income levels for families with children, for families without children and for families with children living on different economic levels.

Theoretical frame of reference: Not explicitly expressed. A committee work within an interdisciplinary sociological frame.

Method employed: Based on existing material and research, with no empirical material of its own.

* * *

Dahlen, U., E. Rönmark & S. Thiberg (1975). *Barnen och den fysiska miljön*/Children and the Physical Environment. SOU 1975:36. Stockholm: Socialdepartementet. Rapport nr. 6 från Barnmiljöutredningen.

Summary: How do children gain access to information about the living conditions of adults and their work. How do they come into contact with adults and old people with different cultural and social views, with steady physical environments, where they can avoid insecurity and obtain continuity, and with an environment that is at their disposal according to their own interest and intention together with adults.

Socialization of Young Children in The Nordic Countries

Theoretical frame of reference: A developmental psychological approach, within which the child is seen as part of a social system, where it functions together with other children and adults. The functioning of the physical environment is assessed in relation to developmental goals.

Method employed: Based on literary studies, experiences from earlier research into housing conditions, field research, contacts with researchers, personnel and institutions, parents, youngsters and children. The material has not been presented in the form of traditional research, but has been presented as a "problem orientated holistic view".

Results: The most effective measures for improving children's living conditions are of a common political character and concern the fundamental distribution of political power. 1. By improving the citizens' influence on the environment through decentralisation of organisations; by improving the active participation of the citizens in common activities by way of distributing rooms and grounds to groups and by supporting activities aimed at children and youngsters. By improving the integration of housing and working areas and by counteracting segregation tendencies in society as a whole. By improving the daily and active contacts between children and adults, via the introduction of a 6-hour working day, regular working hours, shorter distances to places of work and through opening the institutions to others than the children. By improving the influence of the distributive agencies and the citizens on decisions higher up, and through better exploitation of the experience of those taking part in the environmental activities.

* * *

Dencik, L. (1985). *Barndomsutveckling och välfärdsutveckling. Forskning om barns välfärd i de nordiska länderna.*/Child Development and Development of The Welfare State. Research on Children's Well-being in The Nordic Countries. In *Barn i Sverige och världen*, pp. 24-45. Norrköping: Utbildningsreproduktion. In Swedish.

Summary: A report on two comparative studies, the FRASBO-project (The French-Swedish childcare projekt) and the BASUN-project (An investigation on Childhood, Society, and Development in the five Nordic countries), focusing on the implications of the societal transformations in Sweden and the other Nordic countries on the everyday-life and socialisation of preschool children.

Theoretical frame of reference: Both projects are conceived of within a socio-ecological model stressing an holistic approach and seaking for contextually based explanations.

Method employed: An analysis of descriptive demographic and sociological data in combination with qualitative data based on interviews with caregivers and observations of children in their natural settings.

Results: It is found that the work-conditions of the parents have a decisive function in structuring the children's socialisation process. The notion "dual-socialisation" is introduced to capture the fact that in modern childhood many children have to oscilate between at least two altering "sociotopes" that have an interaction rather than a direct effect on the children's well-being. Furthermore it is concluded that the continuous and rapid pace by which changes in Nordic societies take place put parents and upbringers in a situation of "chronic perplexity" with respect to what to do with the young ones. Tendencies to "parental abdication" in combination with professionalisation and pedagogisation of the everyday-life of the young children are noted.

* * *

Förkortad *arbetstid för småbarnsföräldrar*/Reduced Working Hours for Parents With Young Children. SOU 1975:62. Stockholm: Socialdepartementet. ISBN 91-38-02458-6. In Swedish.

Summary: A statement by the Committee of Family Support. The commission was charged with the task of finding ways to prolong maternity leave so that parents with young children would be able to work reduced hours for a longer period than the presently allotted 8 months, before their right to parental payment lapses. The committee has also considered the influence of such a system the parents' position on the labour market and the chances of a reduction of irregular working hours.

Theoretical frame of reference: Not explicitly expressed. A committee work within a sociological frame.

Method employed: Based on existing empirical data and material.

Results: The committee recommends a prolongation of paid maternal leave combined with the establishment of rules about a sharing of the leave between the parents. This should enable the parents to reduce their working day to 6 hours with parental payment for a longer period than is the case at present. The committee also proposes an improvement of the support given when the child is ill. Furthermore, the question of job security is treated. An extension of the childcare system and of the parental leave system is seen as an essential condition of a more child-friendly society.

* * *

Insulander, E. (1975). *Barnen och betongen. En rapport om barns villkor i en svensk förort*/Children and the Concrete. A Report about the Conditions of Children In a Swedish Suburb. Stockholm: LiberFörlag. ISBN 91-38-02067-x. In Swedish.

Summary: A survey of the physical and social environment of children living in Rosingård; a typical housing area built in the 1960ies in Malmö, with about 20,000 inhabitants.

Theoretical frame of reference: Not explicitly expressed but a sociological approach based on empirical data.

Method employed: Qualitative survey with interviews with 68 adults and 53 children between 5-13 years, both Swedish and immigrants. Observations of how often the children and the adults were together, how often the children played with each other and of how the children made use of the physical environment, of toys and so on.

Results: Children and parents are in need of societal support in excess of what they already receive from the school and the preschool. The town planners and the planners of housing areas must give more consideration to the development of children and the direct requirements that this development places upon the physical and social environment. Improved possibilities for contacts between children, youngsters and adults must be established such as indoor and outdoor meeting places that can develop, stimulate and enrich organised activities and closer contacts among those working for a richer environment.

* * *

Lindberg, G. & I. Sjöberg (1981). *Levnadsförhållanden. Rapport nr. 21. Om barns villkor*/Living Conditions. Report no. 21. About Childrens' Conditions. Stockholm: LiberFörlag/Allmänna Förlaget. ISBN 91-38-06637-8. In Swedish.

Summary: Presents the frames for and the living conditions of children, how families with children are composed and parents' working and housing conditions. A comparison of the living conditions of the children of unskilled workers and those of skilled workers, of the children of immigrants, of natives and of Swedish natives and of children living in residential neighbourhoods and those living in blocks of flats is also presented.

Theoretical frame of reference: Not explicitly expressed, but a sociological approach with importance attached to the empirical side.

Method employed: Based on Statistiska Centralbyrån's survey of living conditions, 1977, a qualitative survey of a sample of persons between 16 and 74 years old and their spouses/common-law husband/wife.

Results: There were 0.8 millions 0-15 year-olds. 190,000 were living in one-parent families. Most of the children belonged to working-class families, the second biggest group to employee families. In most of the families, at least one of the parents had more than a primary school education. In 1/6 of the families at least one of the parents was an immigrant. 2/3 of the children lived in residential neighbourhoods, in villas, or town-houses. 1/10 lived in blocks of flats, with at least 4 rooms. If the mother was a single breadwinner, the family seldom lived in residential neighbourhoods. 1/10 of the children lived in very small flats. 0.1 million children had cohabiting parents, both working. Usually the father worked full-time and the mother part-time. 17% of the children had parents who both worked full-time. The mothers took care of most of the housework, even if they worked full-time. Half of the preschool children had one of the parents at home during the day. About 1/3 of the preschool children were in public daycare. If both parents worked or studied about half of the preschool children were in daycare. 1/6 of the 7-10 year-olds were in public daycare, youth centres or childminding. 1/6 managed alone for part of the day. Less than 1/4 of the municipal daycare places were occupied by 7-10 year-olds, whose parents both worked or studied. Parents of school children were often active in associations. 28%, mostly the mothers, were active in parental associations. Single breadwinners complained more often of tiredness, headaches and sleeplessness. More than half of the children had parents who smoked, mostly belonging to the working class. Children from working class families, immigrant families and children living in blocks of flats lived under poorer conditions than children of skilled workers, of Swedish parents and children living in a residential neighbourhood.

* * *

Näsman, E., K. Nordström & R. Hammarström (1983). *Föräldrars arbete & Barns villkor - en kunskapsöversikt.*/The Parents' Work & Children's Conditions - an Overview of Knowledge. Stockholm: LiberFörlag. ISSN 0348-7210. In Swedish.

Summary: A survey of how the parents' working conditions influence the conditions of children in today's Sweden. The following are some of the themes focussed in the survey: The long working hours of fathers to young children, mothers' part-time job and the parents irregular working hours, how wage conditions influence economic freedom of action, how one acts as a parent after a long day at a busy one-sided job, how the different possibilities for influencing ones work situation effect the way one treats one's children, how unemployment influences the family and the children.

Theoretical frame of reference: Not explicitly expressed, but within a sociological frame.

Method employed: Based on existing material within the areas of working life and children's research.

* * *

Mårtensson, S. (1979). *On the Formation of Biographies in Space-Time Environments.* Lund: Gleerup, 1979. Lund studies in geography, Series B, 47. ISBN 91-40-04720-2. In English.

Summary: Analysis of the relationship between environmental structure and the growth of individual biographies. 3 case studies have been undertaken in which the effects of societal organisation are studied. The problem areas concern relocation of a workplace, differences in living conditions within and between regions, and public childcare for preschool children. The distribution of action possibilities between categories of inhabitants is analysed, thus yielding conclusions about, for instance, the networks of contractors that are feasible with a particular societal structure, and the opportunities for the formation of biographies for various categories within a population.

Theoretical frame of reference: A study undertaken with the approach conceptual apparatus and descriptive methods of time-geography, that stresses the interwoven character of events and situation in daily life, as this has been developed within the research group for process and system analysis in human geography at Lund University.

Method Employed: 3 case studies based on existing empirical data.

* * *

Reimer, I. (1975). *Barn och föräldrars arbete*/Children and Their Parents' Work. SOU 1975:37. Stockholm: Socialdepartementet. ISBN 91-38-02247-8. In Swedish.

Summary: An illustration of parents' working conditions and of how the children's lives are influenced by the parents' work.

Theoretical frame of reference: Not explicitly expressed, but a sociologically directed approach.

Method employed: Based on existing empirical data and material describing the conditions today. A committee work.

Results: The existing material indicates unambiguously that children in Sweden are in a tight spot. There is not enough time and energy for them, and perhaps also lack of real interest. But there are signs of a possible reversal. People are beginning to realise, that production and consumption have been too much in focus. This is in favour of the "non-productive" children among others.

* * *

Rydin, I. (1982). *Fakta om barn i Sverige*/Facts About Children in Sweden. Stockholm: Akademi Litteratur. ISBN 91-7410-159-5. In Swedish.

Summary: A collocation of facts, committee works and research about the situation of children in today's Sweden.

Theoretical frame of reference: Not explicitly expressed, but based on existing empirical material.

Method employed: An analysis of existing research and material.

* * *

YOUNG CHILDREN'S SOCIAL CONDITIONS

Andersson, B.-E. (1985). *Familjerna och barnomsorgen*/Families and Childcare. FAST-projektet 36. Stockholm: Högskolan för Lärarutbilding i Stockholm. Institutionen för pedagogik. Rapport, 5. ISBN 91-7656-096-1. In Swedish. With an English summary.

Summary: A study of changes in the family, of public childcare and how the parents make use of and experience this.

Theoretical frame of reference: Within the ecology of human development, where the developmental process is seen as a function of correlation between the developing individual and its environment.

Method employed: Based on interviews with 128 families in Gothenburg and Stockholm.

Results: More than 70% of families with children belong to the category nuclear families. Included in this category are families where the parents are cohabiting. Less than 1/5 are single parent families. For families with young children, the number is less. The average duration of a marriage is more than 11 years. The families, where the parents are cohabiting and not married, are not as stable as the families where the parents are married. 80% of the children in single parent families have experienced at least one change in the family status, for example, a divorce or a separation. In the two-parent families, the number is only 15%. Most parents seem to be satisfied with their childcare. There are no differences in the judgment of the different kinds of childcare. This indicates that an enlarged childcare system will give the parents better possibilities for choosing the kind of childcare that they prefer. Where the children are 6-7 years old, the parents prefer a part-time preschool.

* * *

Socialization of Young Children in The Nordic Countries

Andersson, I. (1979). *Tankestilar och hemmiljö. En uppföljning av barns utveckling från 1-12 år*/Thinking Styles and Home Environment. A Follow-Up Study of Children's Development from 1-12 Years. Göteborg: Acta Universitatis Gothenburgensis, 1979. ISBN 91-7346-061-3. ISSN 0436-1121. In Swedish. With an English summary.

Summary: A follow-up study of a group of children from infancy until they were 12 years old. The purpose of this study is to investigate and interpret the interaction between variables in the children's home environment and their cognitive development. This is achieved by assessing children's cognitive level at the age of twelve, by describing the behaviour and home background, by analysing the relationship between the psychological measurements and the cognitive level, by investigating to what extent different conditions in the home environment can explain the cognitive level and by studying the relationship between cognitive level and the children's behaviour. For example, peer orientation, school adjustment, school achievement and self-evaluation.

Theoretical frame of reference: Within the frames of the psychological thoughts and theories of Bernstein and Liljeström and Piaget's theories about the principles and drives of cognitive development.

Method employed: In 1963, a randomly choosen group of 480 children aged 1 month to 2 years was tested in motoric, personal, social, vocabulary, performance and specific hand-eye coordination skills. 298 were tested when they were between 4 and 5 years old and finally, 242 at the age of 12, when the cognitive and social development were highlighted. The children's perception of their home environment was also measured with respect to involvement in nice activities, parent-school contact and the parents' method of rearing. Based on tests of the children, questionnaires of the parents and children.

Results: An overview of the home environment and the behaviour of the children is given and comparisons are made concerning differences between sexes and occupational and educational criteria in the groups. The sex differences found, were often related to the parents' education. However, in general, the girls experienced more warmth, more control and more explanations from the mothers, whereas the boys were confronted with high demands to achieve well at school, from both parents. There were considerable variations within the social groups concerning child rearing patterns. The less stimulating home environments, were often found in the educationally least qualified groups. In the 4 year-olds study, there was a high correlation between social groups and child rearing patterns, whereas the 12 year-olds study showed a less apparent connection. In this study there were also some differences between the sexes in social and cognitive development. Girls, in general, were found to have a higher ability in the Swedish and English languages, and were more ambitious and hard working than the boys. There were also educational group differences, concerning social and cognitive behaviour. Children with educationally more qualified parents, showed a higher incidence of abstract thinking, more elaborative use of language and a higher level of marks in school. It was not possible to identify children who could think abstractly at 12 years of age from the results of earlier findings. Concerning the early home environment, the children with the highest scores on the vocabulary test include a high proportion from homes in which the parents have communicated to a great extent, offered explanations, explained prohibitions, read fairy-tales and made books easily available. Caring adults using the language explicitly, is of importance to the cognitive development of the children, just as it is important that parents make demands upon their children, let them take responsibility and let them feel that they are expected to achieve well. Concerning school, there is a very large variation in cognitive level and the school often gives priority to the children's verbal ability at the expense of creative thinking.

* * *

Annerblom, M.-L. (1979). *Dagisfröken - barnvakt eller pedagog? Om könsroller och samarbetsproblem*/Nursery Governess - Child Supervisor or Pedagogue? About Sex-roles and Co-operational Problems. Stockholm: Wahlström & Widstrand. ISBN 91-46-13481-6. In Swedish.

Socialization of Young Children in The Nordic Countries

Summary: A description of the sex-role changes of preschool teachers and of how this group experienced the need for change and the kind of changes to be made.

Theoretical frame of reference: Within a feministic frame based on the theories of Paulo Freire.

Method employed: Participant observations, interviews and diary records in a daycare centre with 60 middle class 1-7 year-olds.

Results: The environment of the daycare centre seems too totally child-centred, with no room for the needs of the adults. The enviroment is planned in a way that invites, familiarising with the traditional woman's role. One of the biggest problems related to the sex-role pattern of the daycare centre, is the absence of men. Usually one of the boys takes over the leading "man's-role" and by this influences the other boys in a way that strengthens aggressive "man-like" behaviour. If the patterns in a group are to be changed, it is necessesary to concentrate on the children, who are taken for models. There were many co-operational problems in the daycare centre, which turned out to be rooted in the generation gap, where the older and the younger generations had opposite ideals. Whereas the older nursery teachers saw themselves first and foremost as caregivers, the younger ones saw themselves as teachers with pedagogical aims. It seems that what influenced the behaviour was the personality and the personnels' "womans-role", rather than their work-role. For further results, reference must be made to the book.

* * *

Armbruster, U., M. Alvesson & A.-M. Begler (red.) *Barn & ungdom. Vardagsvillkor och Samhällsomsorg. En fragmentarisk kunskapsöversikt*/Children and Youth. Everyday Conditions and Social Welfare. A Fragmentary Survey of Knowledge. Stockholm: Forsknings- och utvecklingsbyrån. Barn & Ungdom, Rapport, nr. 4. ISSN 0283-1481. In Swedish.

Summary: The aim of the survey has been to create a basis within the field of childhood and youth that can give a general picture of 1) the state of knowledge about the conditions of everyday life, the organisational-, work- and developmental conditions of the social service personnel and 2) the meeting between children, youth and parents, on the one side and the social service personnel and others, on the other. To this end approaches are given, important literature indicated and other surveys presented.

Theoretical frame of reference: Not explicitly expressed.

Method employed: Based on existing surveys within the field of childhood and youth and complemented by a comprehensive selection of literature, reports, etc.

* * *

Bäckström, C., [et al.] (1985). *Jordgubbsbarnen på dagis. Om barnens sociala liv på en syskonavdelning*/On the Social Life of the Children in an Age-Integrated Daycare Group. Stockholm: Forsknings- och utvecklingsbyrän, Stockholms socialförvaltning, Rapport nr. 21. In Swedish.

Summary: A very detailed description and analysis of the children's social interactions with each other and with the staff in a daycare group. The children are between 2.6 and 6.0 years of age.

Theoretical frame of reference: A social interactionist perspective within the frames of a socio-ecological model.

Method employed: Extensive interviews with parents and care-givers at the daycare centres combined with systematic long-term observations of the social interaction-pattern of each individual child in the daycare group.

Results: The children have frequent and many short interaction-sequences with each other. Activities of different kinds take place simultaneously in the setting. Quick shifts and many interruptions characterise the social life in the group. Children of the same age prefer each other as playmates. The younger children turn to each other, rather than to the staff-members when making references to their own family or to other experiences outside the daycare centre, rather than any individual child or the staff-members, appears to be the most influential point of reference at the daycare for the children. More than anything the children seem to strive to conform their own behaviour to what appears to be the group norm.

The children do not interact frequently with members of the staff. When they do, it is often to seek help with something the child cannot manage itself. When a staff-member relates to a child it is very often in order to discourage something the child does. The staff-members oscilate between a role of octopus-like helpers and passive supervisers to the children.

* * *

Björklid, P. (1982). *Children's Outdoor Environments. A Study of Children's Outdoor Activities on Two Housing Estates, From the Perspective of Environmental and Developmental Psychology.* Lund: CWK Gleerup, 1982. ISBN 91-40-04815-2. In English.

Summary: A demonstration of the consequences of a narrowly planned outdoor environment and suggestions for the design of the outdoor environment.

Theoretical frame of reference: Within theories of developmental (J. Piaget, E. H. Erikson & H. H. Mead), ecological and environmental psychology, with the emphasis placed on the reciprocal nature of the man-environment relationship.

Method employed: Based on empirical data concerning children's outdoor activities on two housing estates.

Results: Mainly older preschool children and younger schoolboys made use of the open spaces on the housing estates. The different designs of the play areas were reflected in the children's interactions with their environment, insofar as activities were more varied on the more diverse and natural estate than on the more "synthetic" one. High-rise buildings, traffic, lack of attractive play areas close at hand and bad weather, are factors in the physical environment that restrict young children's and girls' outdoor play, in particular. An indirect social factor which impedes mainly young children's outdoor interactions, is a lack of suitable activities for adults. Two recommendations are made: To set aside all open spaces on housing estate for play and to provide playgrounds with play-leaders on housing estates.

* * *

Bra *daghem för små barn* (1981)/Good Daycare for Young Children. Stockholm: Socialdepartementet, (SOU) 1981:25. ISBN 91-38-06/68-0. ISSN 0375-250X. In Swedish. With an English summary.

Summary: In the report, the Family Aid Commission describes prerequisites and present proposals concerning provision of good daycare, of attending day-nurseries and of family daycare.

Theoretical frame of reference: Not explicitly expressed, but within the frames of psychological theories of young children's social and emotional development.

Method employed: Based on existing research and material.

Results: Regarding young children in society, the Family Aid Commission suggests: That childcare is expanded according to the aims decided upon by parliament in 1976 that priority is given in the expansion to childcare for the youngest children and that it is organised in such a way that parents working irregular hours can make use of it. Regarding research on children in childcare: That a preschool council be established which, among other things, is given the opportunity to found an institution for child research and to allocate funds for preschool pedagogical research. Regarding good daycare for small children: That the municipalities are encouraged to include a description of the quality of childcare in their childcare planning. Regarding development of the pedagogical work: That the authorities concerned be directed to compile an overview of the educational level of child nurses, preschool teachers, staff of free time centres and family daycare mothers, with the purpose of raising the quality of education. Regarding problems in society: That a preschool commission be established with the function of allocating resources to housing areas with special problems. Regarding pedagogics and preschool programs: That the staff within the area of childcare, plans and evaluates their work, that politicians and parents together with the staff participate, that further education is carried on with the aim of continuously developing and increasing knowledge about the role of the heads of daycare centres and preschools, that the municipalities point out the need to introduce more everyday activities in the pedagogical work and considers this when planning the environment. Regarding young children in groups: That a more concious effort is made to develop and make use of the particular possibilities offered by the group, that even the small children are given the possibility to develop playing together and that knowledge about adults and children in groups be increased. Regarding starting preschool or family daycare: That every child starting preschool or family daycare be given an introduction suited to the child's needs, that immigrant children be given bilingual staff as well as a longer period of introduction. Regarding mixed age groups: That research and developmental work concering mixed age groups be initiated, followed and evaluated and that the knowledge in this area be increased in the education of preschool teachers, staff of free time centres and child nurses. Regarding parent participation: That the municipalities be given the task of starting, following up and evaluating research projects regarding parental participation in daycare centres, that material is developed as a guide for proposed projects, that problems in reference to employment legalities, economy and insurance with parental participation be quickly investigated and that the importance of parental participation be treated in the education programmes. Regarding family daycare: That family daycare mothers be given the opportunity to work in groups and to co-operate with the rest of the preschool activity, that they reach a level of competence that can be compared to the basic eduction of child nurses (6 months), that they can take part in continuing further education, that they receive an introduction to the work as is the case in other areas of childcare that they are given better opportunities for pedagogical guidance that developmental work within family daycare be initiated and that the municipality draw up an account of quality demands that apply to family daycare and what efforts are made to fulfil these. Regarding the health of young children in daycare: that routines are developed in order to discover the children with medical/psychological problems that are in need of special support and stimulation, that plans are made to follow up and if needed, to ensure treatment of these children, that the needs be documented and used as a basis for the planning, that this area become an urgent area for research and development and finally, that epidemics, infections and allergic diseases should be followed.

* * *

Dahlberg, G. (1985). *Context and the Child's Orientation to Meaning. A Study of the Child's Way of Organizing the Surrounding World in Relation to Public, Institutionalized Socialization.* Lund: CWK Gleerup, 1985. ISBN 91-40-05120-x. In English.

Summary: An illumination of the processes which are operating when children from different social backgrounds are met by the world of public socialisation. Two main issues have been considered: (1) the relationship between the child's orientation to meaning and her/his family's social background and (2) the relationship between the child's orientation to meaning and the transmission processes and practices of public socialisation.

Theoretical frame of reference: Within a contextual perspective, (grounded in Piaget's developmental theory, Bernstein's theory of cultural reproduction and Lundgren's theory on education and reproduction processes), in which the child's way of relating to the surrounding world is viewed as a form of encounter between historical and structual conditions and action on different levels. An empirically based study.

Method employed: Based on interviews with 135 children, who where asked to classify different occupations.

Results: Children whose parents have a high position in society, have a tendency to produce context-independent rationales, while children whose parents have a low position, have a tendency to produce context-dependent rationales. The children who produce context-independent orientation to meaning, stand in a closer relation to preschool and school by displaying more of an official pedagogical competence. The implication of the institutionalisation of the child's socialisation, even at younger ages, when more of the child's time and space is regulated by public socialisation, is discussed.

* * *

Dencik, L. [et al.] (1985). *Dagisbarn och hemmabarn i Frasbo*/Children in daycare and children reared at home in Frasbo. In *Kritisk Utbildningstidskrift, Nr. 1, 1985, pp. 42-53.* In Swedish.

Summary: A report on findings from a study of preschoolers' interaction with their caregivers in a typical Stockholm suburb. One part of the children spend their days in a public daycare centre, another part spend their days at home with their mother.

Theoretical frame of reference: A socio-ecological model in which the attention is focussed on the impact of the structural conditions of the settings on the social interaction-pattern between the parties present in the settings.

Method employed: Systematic long-term observations of the social interaction-pattern of individual children in their natural settings.

Results: Considerable differences are found with respect to how adults and children relate to each other in the two settings. In the daycare centres individual children and staff members do not interact very much at all, and when they do the social interactions are on the whole of an instrumental character. Affective manifestations are rare, the care-giving has a "mechanic" flavour. Children are not given individual attention, but are treated as if they were equals with respect to abilities and interests - even if they as a matter of fact differ considerably in terms of age, background, etc. Children who spend their days at home with their mother, on the contrary, are in close continuous verbal and physical interactions with her. Mothers are very attentative even to subtle signals from their child and understand them adequately. There are frequent affective manifestations of varying kinds from both parties. Children in this type of care have few social contacts with other children and adults.

* * *

Ekholm, B., M. Ekholm & A. Hedin (1982). *Baggrund och mätinstrument*/The Climate in Daycare Centres. Theoretical Background and Methods of Measurement. Linköping: Pedagogiska Institutionen. Rapport LiU-PEK-R-79. ISBN 91-7372-582-x. In Swedish.

Summary: The present study focuses on the total climate of daycare centres and its effect on children's social and emotional behaviour.

Theoretical frame of reference: A theoretical model for analysing the daycare centre climate, has been developed.

Method employed: Observations of children and personnel interaction in 12 daycare centres, quantitative interviews with personnel and children and measurements of the attitudes of the children.

Results: Development of a multi-method model for measurement of the child rearing climate in daycare centres.

* * *

Elmelind-Hedblom, A.-C. & I. Ivermark (1983). *Sambandsstudie av pedagogisk arbetssätt och barns målriktade beteende på dagis*/A Study of the Connection Between Pedagogical Working Method and Children's Goal-Directed Behaviour in Daycare Centres. Uppsala: Uppsala Universitet, PEG-Uppsats HT. In Swedish.

Summary: A study of connections between the pedagogical working method of the personnel and the children's goal-directed behaviour. Here the goal-directed behaviour is defined as "being capable of setting aims for conduct, to realise them in different ways and to continue conduct until the aim has been reached". The child's development is influenced by both biological factors and by the social environment. In this study, the social environment is more precisely the pedagogy that the child meets in the institution.

Theoretical frame of reference: Not explicitly expressed, but a sociological approach based on empirical data.

Method employed: Survey based on empirical data gathered in 1982 in 6 daycare institutions in Uppsala. Quantitative interviews, activity-analysis, observations and tests.

Results: On the basis of the centres' advance planning of activities, it was possible to effect their division into structured and unstructured centres. There were 2 structured centres. Both goal-directed and non-goal-directed behaviour occurred more in the structured than in the unstructured centres.

* * *

Fagerström, E. (1976). *Barn. En sammanfattning av barnmiljöutredningen*/Children. A Summary of the Elucidation of the statement of Children's Environmental Conditions. Stockholm: LiberFörlag, 1976. ISBN 91-38-03158-2. In Swedish.

Summary: A survey of the situation of the child in Sweden today. Among other things, the development and rearing of the child, the situation of families with children, the influence of working life on the children, children's housing conditions and childcare are looked into.

* * *

Gunnarsson, L. (1984). *Fädrars och mödrars informella sociala nätverk. Resultat från en intervjuundersökning*/The Informal Social Network of Fathers and Mothers. Results From an Interview Survey.

FAST-projektet, 22. Gothenburg: Göteborgs Universitet. Institutionen för praktisk pedagogik. Rapport, 134. ISSN: 0348-2219.

Summary: "Family Support and Development" is the title of the Swedish part of a cross-national research project. The personal social network, meaning the parents' contacts with relatives, neighbours, friends, work-mates and other people in the environment, is examined. Different aspects of this network are related to some background factors; especially to the job status and the sex of the parents.

Theoretical frame of reference: An analysis of the personal social network, a description of procedures for developing an interview instrument to analyse the quantity and quality of contacts.

Method employed: A longitudinal study. Data were collected over a period of 5 years. Interviews with 166 couples, where the results of the interviews with the fathers were compared to those of the mothers.

Results: Contacts with relatives came to 45%, with friends 37% and with neighbours 18%. The network of the working-class families is more relatively orientated than that of the middle class families (52% versus 39%). The women have more contact to their relatives than the men, they also have closer contact to their neighbours. There are differences in areas, where the number of working class families and immigrants is high. The number of friends is higher in middle class families than in working class families.

* * *

Jorup, B. (1979). *Lekens pedagogiske möjligheter. En analys av barns lek på daghem utifrån Jean Piagets teori*/The Educational Potentials of Play. An analysis of Children's Play in Daycare Centres Based on Piaget's Theory. Stockholm: Gotab, 1979. ISBN 91-7146-035-7. In Swedish, with an English summary.

Socialization of Young Children in The Nordic Countries

Summary: An investigation of the educational potentials of play in daycare, in relation to child development and education and of the fruitfulness of Piaget's theory in relation to play.

Theoretical frame of reference: Within the frames of Jean Piaget's theory of development and play.

Method employed: Based on semistructured systematic observations of four groups of small children aged 6 months to 2 1/2 years, five sibling groups aged 2 1/2 to 7 years, and on interviews with the teachers in the children's groups.

Results: In the group of small children, practice play is by far the dominating form of play, whereas, in the sibling groups, symbol play dominates. Spontaneous games with rules and without adult participation were very rare. It was difficult to categorise the observations according to form of play. Verbal contact was noticed in 71% of the observations of contact in the groups of small children and in 91% of the sibling groups. In this group, there is little difference between use of verbal contact in practice and symbol play, whereas there is considerable difference in the groups of small children. The children more often imitate each other, than they imitate the teachers. Playing provides good opportunities for concept formation and the accommodation and assimilation of language. By using a specific competence in play, the child not only further develops that competence, but also develops his/her potential for a more general competence. The author is sceptical about the concept of "free" play, but prefers the concept "liberating" play, in relation to the concept of competence. Good play is play that provides the child with situations in which he/she can test his/her own resources. What kind of activity the child engages in and the content of his/her play is not without importance.

* * *

Kärrby, G. *Utveckling i grupp. Socialisationsprocessen i förskolan*/Development in Groups. The Socialisation Process in

Preschool. Stockholm: Liber Läromedel. ISBN 91-47-02226-4. In Swedish.

Summary: A study of the interaction between teachers and children and of how the children are influenced by different factors in preschool, of which factors influence the social development of children, how they adapt social attitudes and values and how much the home and the preschool, respectively, influence this.

Theoretical frame of reference: Not explicitly expressed, but within a sociological frame.

Method employed: Based on interviews, conversations and observations from the project "The Process of Socialisation in Preschool" and other research.

Results: With no final results, but a presentation of interpretations, views and proposals. An all-round description of everyday life in the preschool.

* * *

Kärrby, G. (1983). *Utvecklingsarbete och administrativ styrning inom förskoleverksamheten*/Developmental Work and Administration of the Preschool. Projektet samordning mellan förskola och övriga familjestödjande organ. Tynneredsprojektet. Gothenburg: Göteborg Universitet. Institutionen för praktisk pedagogik. Rapport, 124. ISSN 0348-2219. In Swedish.

Summary: A presentation and analysis of aims and instructions for the social administration regarding the activities of the preschool, with a view to changing the intended direction.

Theoretical frame of reference: Not explicitly expressed, but within an organisational explanatory model divided into structural, normative and subjective levels.

Method employed: A quantitative survey based on committee work, active observation and interviews.

Results: The preschool is interpreted as a social political resource. The interpretation of the conception of coordination as an organisational principle in administration, is being related to coordination as a pedagogical conception. Decentralisation, what the establishment of preschool secretariats was supposed to promote, resulted in a new link in line organisation and seems to function more as a control organ than as a pedagogical resource. This could be because the in-service education of the secretariats mostly included administrative knowledge. The results of developmental work concerning economic self management in the institutions, resulted first and foremost in more conscious decision-making among the personnel. Any effects on the pedagogical work could not be seen. In reality, the organisational and administrative changes that were made to coordinate and decentralise the preschool activities had no decisive effects on the pedagogical work. It can be assumed that the structures and valuation system that characterise organisations, is typical for the changes. Correlations between a pedagogical and organisational/administrative perspective have been made on an ideological level.

* * *

Lamb, M. [et al.] (In press). *Determinants of Social Competence in Swedish Pre-Schoolers*. Research paper. Reprints request to M. E. Lamb, Department of Psychology, University of Utah, Salt Lake City, UT 84112, USA. In English. With an English summary.

Summary: A study of the effects of the quality of family and daycare centres on firstborn Swedish children from socio-economically diverse backgrounds, including the design measures of family background characteristics and pre-enrollment measures of relevant child characteristics.

Theoretical frame of reference: Not explicitly expressed, but a strongly directed empirical sociological approach.

Method employed: A sample of 140 firstborn Swedish children, at the average of 16 month of age, all on the waiting list for a place in a daycare centre. 53 were admitted to a daycare centre, 33 to family daycare and 54 remained at home with their parents. Interviews with parents and observations of the children. Follow-up assessments one year after the initial interviews and observations.

Results: Type and quality of non-familial childcare, had no significant effect on these aspects of child development. The major determinant of personality maturity were background variables, high family SES, high quality of home care, and easy temperament facilitated personality maturity. Availability of support from maternal grandparents had a smaller, but significant effect. Prior social skills and age were the best predictors of peer social skills evidenced on the post-test.

* * *

Larsson, E. [et al.] (1984). *Blåbärsbarnen på dagis. Om barnens social liv på en småbarns avdelning.*/On the Social Life of the Children in a Group of Toddlers in a Daycare Centre. Stockholm: Forsknings- och utvecklingsbyrån, Stockholms socialförvaltning, Rapport nr. 20. In Swedish.

Summary: A very detailed description and analysis of the children's social interactions with each other and with the staff in a daycare group. The children are between 1.1 and 3.1 years of age.

Theoretical frame of reference: A social interactionist perspective within the frames of a socio-ecological model.

Method employed: Extensive interviews with parents and caregivers at the daycare centres combined with systematic long-term observations of the social interaction-pattern of each individual child in the daycare group.

Results: These children spent more time by themselves than in interaction with each other. They did not engage in any cooperative play-activities. The children were more engaged in watching each other, "gazing", than in actually interacting. Interactions, when they occurred between the children, were hasty and mostly non-verbal.

The children and the staff-members did not interact except in situations that clearly demanded that. It is concluded that the notion of "social interaction" in fact is a misnomer for what actually goes on between staff and children - which is rather a kind of one-way communication in which one party acts and the other party re-acts without further comments. Mostly it is the children who acts and the staff that re-acts.

* * *

Lissell, B. (1985). *Mödras och barns gemensamma aktiviteter - resultat från en intervjuundersökning i FAST-projektet*/Mothers and Children's Common Activities - Results From an Interview Survey in Connection With the FAST-project. Stockholm: Högskolan för lärarutbilding i Stockholm. Institutionen för pedagogik, Rapport, 6/Barnpsykologiska Forskningsgruppen: FAST-projektet, 37. ISBN 91-7656-097-X, ISSN 0348-4335. In Swedish.

Summary: A study of how the common activities of mothers and their 3-4 year old children vary dependent on conditions of the ecological environment. The relations to the child can be seen from different socialisation- and child rearing perspectives, and comparisons are made, among other things, of family type, work background and whether they work in the home or outside.

Theoretical frame of reference: Within an ecological model of human development (Bronfenbrenner) based on both cognitive and social psychological aspects.

Method employed: Quantitative, loose structured interviews with 128 city families about the routines and activities constituting their everyday life.

Results: Among other things: About half of the children who were at home on a fairly usual day, went shopping and made excursions with their mothers. Just as many meet family, friends and neighbours. The children in daycare during the day were together with their mothers just as much as the "home children". They participated in the housework, saw T.V., were read to and so on. The mothers engaged in different activities together with girls and boys. On holidays it was usual to see family and friends, to make excursions and to be outside in the woods and the fields. 1/3 of the families were very active during holidays and just as many preferred only one type of holiday activity, or none at all.

* * *

Noren-Björn, E. (1980). *Förskolepedagogik i praktiken. Vuxenstyrd, barnstyrd, materialstyrd eller...*/Preschool Pedagogy in Practice. Ruled by Adults, Children, Materials or... Lund: Liber Läromedel, 1980. ISBN 91-40-30407-8. In Swedish.

Summary: A discussion of whether adults, children, environment or materials, rule the preschool, and whether it is the standard of the localities, the multitude of the materials or other factors that are decisive for whether a preschool is functioning pedagogically well.

Theoretical frame of reference: Not explicitly expressed, but within a sociological frame and based on empirical data.

Method employed: Based on a combination of participant and direct observations of 7 groups of children from 7 different preschools; one group of children aged 6 months to 2 1/2 years the other groups aged 2 years 5 month to 10 years. Also, interviews with the personnel regarding the children's play and their interaction with the adults. Futhermore, the personnels' dairy notes have been evaluated and a continuous discussion with the personnel about materials, working methods and the children has been carried on.

Results: Today, there is a strong belief in the importance of the environment and the material and less understanding of the importance of the adults' roles in creating the best opportunities in the preschool. The interaction of children and adults is of the greatest importance and affects the children and by this, all the activities. For specific results, reference must be made to the book.

* * *

Schyl-Bjurman, G. (1982). *Central intention och lokal verklighet. Pedagogisk implementering av et centralt utarbetet målprogram. En fallstudie*/Central Intention and Local Reality. Pedagogical Implementation of a Centrally Prepared Programme of Goals. A Case Study. Lund: LiberFörlag, 1982. ISBN 91-38-60026-9. In Swedish. With an English Summary.

Summary: A study of a preschool educational programme drawn up by the 1968 Preschool Committee. The program was tested in five municipalities. Only one is tested here, which was confined to three daycare centres in Smalltown. The study describes and endeavours to explain the interaction between the people involved when an experiment is initiated, takes shape and is concluded.

Theoretical frame of reference: Based on the theory of the sociology of knowledge and the theory of symbolic interaction.

Method employed: Based on detailed interviews with project leader, politicians, administrative officers, daycare centre staff and parents.

Results: When a policy drawn up at central government level is to be implemented in educational practice, the aim and the purposes should be expressed as unambigously as possible, thus making it possible to co-ordinate method, educational efforts and local decisions with this aim and what underlies it. The practical implementation of educational theory takes place in a social setting containing status hierarchies, power structures and institutionalised types of behaviour. Unless these factors are considered, the experiment may be slowed down or arouse passive resistance, because it is considered a presumptive threat.

* * *

Svenning, C. & M. Svenning (1979). *Daghemmen, jämlikheten och klasssamhället. En studie av skiktspecifik socialisation i det svenska samhället*/Daycare Centres, Equality and Class Society. A Study of Stratified Socialisation in Swedish society. ISBN 91-40-30303-9. In Swedish with an English summary.

Summary: The purpose of the study is to clarify the importance of the daycare for the primary socialisation of children. Emphasis is placed on the developmental and equality-promoting function of the daycare in a society characterised by social stratification and an unfair distribution of resources.

Theoretical frame of reference: Based on a structural-process product-model, where the child is seen as the social product of both the home and the daycare.

Method employed: Quantitative analysis based on interviews with preschool teachers, children and parents, on observations of the children and on documents and records.

Results: It is claimed that the daycare significantly provides no important social complement to the rearing of the home. Daycare is part of the structures contributing to stratified socialisation and to social, economic and political inequality.

* * *

William-Olsson, I., R. Colven & A. Söderlund (1985). *Livet i barnstugorna. En slutrapport från MAFF-projektet*/Life in the Daycare Centres. A Final Report From the MAFF-project. Stockholm: Högskolan för lärarutbildning i Stockholm, Institutionen för pedagogik. Rapport 1. ISBN 91-7657-092-9, ISSN 0348-4335. In Swedish.

Summary: Research aimed at creating continuity for the children through organisational changes in the institution. An evaluation of the MAFF-project (versatile use of preschools and youth centres in the Stockholm area) and of the interdisciplinary research into the problems connected with carrying out the intentions of the project in 5 experimental daycare centres, seen from a pedagogical and architectural point of view.

Theoretical frame of reference: Qualitative and naturalistic research process with pedagogical, architectural and sociological perspectives.

Method employed: Already existing empirical material, consisting of observations, interviews and register data have been analysed and interpreted.

Results: The planning after the project had started, took place in groups with different set-ups and fields of responsibility. The personnel were not able to formulate pedagogical perspectives in excess of everyday life and organisational problems that had to be solved in order to keep everyday life of the institutions functioning free of friction. A lot of time was used to give the activities a distinct form. That the form came to dominate the planning, can be seen as a result of the lack of content and pedagogical perspective. Basis groups of age mixed children (0-12) and cross groups of children of the same age from different basis groups were established. The personnel refused to let the parents have any influence on the planning, so the attempt to create continuity between the home and the daycare centre through the co-operation of the parents in the planning process, was not carried through. However, contacts between the children and adults from the neighbourhood led to a valuable continuity, even if it was not in the form of common planned activities. The personnel had the community inside the centre in view. The children were trained in the community through participating in the work and through gatherings, where they could choose between and decide about activities. Parents and "neighbours" were not allowed into the community. A kind of alternative culture was developed. The children were held responsible and had to show consideration in relatively stable groups. They saw how decisions are made and they took part in the decision-making process. They acquired certain knowledge about the environment through study visits and different topic-related projects.

* * *

Ögren, K. (1980). *Fråga barnen. Om barns liv i två bostadsområden i Örebro*/Ask the Children. About Children's Lives in Two Housing Areas in Örebro. Stockholm: Almqvist & Wiksell International. Statens råd för byggnadsforskning. T 5:1980. ISBN 91-540-3217-2. In Swedish.

Summary: A description of the conditions of 7-12 year-olds in two housing areas in Örebro, made and interpreted by the children themselves.

Theoretical frame of reference: Of a marxist and critical theoretical outlook.

Method employed: Qualitative interviews with children between 7 and 12 years old and with their mothers (35). Interviews with planners of the housing areas (12) and with the personnel of the institutions (21) and observation studies of 3 playgrounds in the area. Population data and the tasks in connection with the physical planning are being analysed.

Results: The housing areas cannot offer the children enough stimulation. The socio-economic and physical conditions are not alike in the different housing areas and intensify the class distinctions in the years when the children grow up. They have no channels through which they can influence their own situation. Because of this, they are dependent on the initiative of their parents and other adults in the physical environments, the daycare and the school. When the wants of the children are not met by the adults, the children are powerless. The children are very isolated from adults and their activities. Demands changes in society, in social planning and in the nearby environment, in sex-roles and in the relationship between adults and children, as well as in the distribution of resources and influence.

* * *

YOUNG CHILDREN'S CULTURAL CONDITIONS

Aronsson, K. [et al.] (1984). *Barn i tid och rum*/The Child in Time and Space. Stockholm: LiberFörlag, 1984. ISBN 91-38-61279-8. In Swedish.

Summary: A survey of current research about children and their conditions with a view to increasing the understanding of the existence of the child, before and now, in Sweden and in other parts of the world.

Theoretical frame of reference: An anthropologically and historically directed approach.

* * *

Ehn, B. (1983). *Ska vi leka tiger? Daghemsliv ur kulturell synsvinkel*/Are We Going to Play Tiger? Daycare Centre Life, From a Cultural Point of View. Lund: LiberFörlag, 1983. ISBN 91-38-60039-0. In Swedish.

Summary: An analysis of the daycare centre from a cultural point of view, seen as a pattern of symbols, conceptions, ideas and values uniting the people within the centre. With a description of children's symbolic animal games, of the irresolution, the confusion of norms and the individualism of the adults concerning rearing, of their striving towards order and structure, of the routines, control, impersonality and the collective adaption. With a perspectivation of the irresolution and order in Swedish culture.

Theoretical frame of reference: An ethnological cultural analysis.

Method employed: Participant observations in 4 socially different daycare centres in 1980-81 and observations from 2 centres, where the author's own children were minded.

* * *

Svenning, C. & M. Svenning (1982). *Mass-media som fostrare*/The Mass-media as Upbringers. Lund: LiberFörlag, 1982. ISBN 91-38-60029-3. In Swedish.

Summary: The authors analyse one week's supply of mass-media and show how children from different environments choose between the different possibilities. The main question is: How do mass-media function as upbringers.

Theoretical frame of reference: Partly a theoretical and partly an empirical exposition.

Method employed: The empirical material consists of a detailed content analysis of 153 TV-programmes and 151 magazines and of material from a subsequent questionnaire of 117 twelve year old children from different social environments and their parents regarding which TV-programmes, radio programmes, pictures, books and so on, they had been occupied with.

Results: Mainly, the children's choices were very much alike. What separated the children, of whom half came from high-rise blocks and the other half from residential neighbourhoods, was the extent of their mass-media consumption. The children from residential neighbourhoods participate to a far higher degree in organised leisure activities and their time for mass-media consumption is limited. Most of the book is devoted to an analysis of the picture of reality in the mass-media. In this reality, women are represented as subordinated to men, workers to other work categories and so on. Mass-media is altogether on the side of the "strong". The reality presented to the children through the mass-media is a reality created by journalists, producers, photographers and so on. This also implies that the children from high-rise blocks acquire a more edited picture of reality, defending particular views of society and personal relations and maintaining a view of inequality among people.

* * *

SUBJECT INDEX

AUTHOR'S INDEX